T0131779

WELCOMING FLOWERS

from across the Cleansed Threshold of Hope

ALSO BY THINLEY NORBU

A Cascading Waterfall of Nectar

*Magic Dance: The Display of the Self-Nature
of the Five Wisdom Dakinis*

*The Small Golden Key to the Treasure of the
Various Essential Necessities of General
and Extraordinary Buddhist Dharma*

*White Sail: Crossing the Waves of Ocean Mind
to the Serene Continent of the Triple Gems*

WELCOMING FLOWERS

from across the Cleansed Threshold of Hope

AN ANSWER TO
POPE JOHN PAUL II'S
CRITICISM OF BUDDHISM

THINLEY NORBU

Shambhala
Boulder
2014

Shambhala Publications, Inc.
2129 13th Street
Boulder, Colorado 80302
www.shambhala.com

©1997 by Thinley Norbu

All rights reserved. No part of this book may be reproduced
in any form or by any means, electronic or mechanical, including
photocopying, recording, or by any information storage and
retrieval system, without permission in writing from the publisher.

Printed in the United States of America

∞ This edition is printed on acid-free paper that meets the
American National Standards Institute z39.48 Standard.
♻ Shambhala Publications makes every effort to print on recycled paper.
For more information please visit www.shambhala.com.

Shambhala Publications is distributed worldwide by
Penguin Random House, Inc., and its subsidiaries.

Library of Congress Cataloging-in-Publication Data

Thinley Norbu.
Welcoming flowers from across the cleansed threshold of hope:
an answer to Pope John Paul II's criticism of
Buddhism/Thinley Norbu.—First Shambhala Edition.
pages   cm
Reprint. Originally published: New York: Jewel Publishing House, ?1997.
Includes bibliographical references.
ISBN 978-1-61180-163-7 (pbk.: alk. paper)
1. Buddhism—Doctrines. 2. Buddhism—Relations—Christianity.
3. Christianity and other religions—Buddhism. 4. John Paul II, Pope,
1920–2005. Varcare la soglia della speranza. I. Title.
BQ4132.T44 2014
294.3′352—dc23
2013030563

CONTENTS

Introduction   1

1. Experience and Enlightenment   5

2. Evil, Good, and Reality   11

3. Breaking Ties to Reality   25

4. Indifference, Detachment, and Love   45

5. Atheism   57

6. Creation   63

7. Union   71

8. Mysticism   81

9. Religions   99

Notes   111

INTRODUCTION

When demons jealously shot harsh, barbed arrows at you,
You responded with soft, delicate flower petals.
When demons brutally fired a thunderous cannon at you,
You abided in the peaceful silence of wisdom samadhi.
You could not even wish to stare at your own jealous
    enemy who hated you.
Protecting beings from horrible samsaric phenomena,
How can we not praise and worship you, the omniscient
    Prince Siddhartha, Buddha Shakyamuni.

—from a Snowland scholar

Recently, the Pope wrote a book called *Crossing the Threshold of Hope,* which has a chapter on Buddhism. I did not know about this book until I received several letters from Poland, from individuals and from a publishing house, asking me to comment on it. When I read the book in order to be able to answer their request, I found that it had serious, gratuitous misrepresentations of Buddhist doctrine that seemed to be based on misunderstandings, though perhaps my own understanding of the chapter is different from the meaning intended by the Pope. So I thought it was necessary to identify and correct these mistakes with clarifications of the Buddhist point of view in order to dispel misconceptions. I have not tried to consider what is generally thought in either traditional or modern Christianity or Catholicism, but only to discuss the Pope's actual words about Buddhism and his comparisons of Christianity to Buddhism.

Of course, the Pope is known as the spiritual leader of millions of Roman Catholics, and his views and opinions are heard around the world. The misinterpretations of Buddhism in his book may have come from listening to advisors who were unfamiliar with Buddhism, from simply glancing at books written at the Hinayana[1] level, or from being shown books by misinformed authors. Perhaps he looked only at negative conceptions about Buddhism written by followers of other doctrines who had malicious intentions, or by idiots who wrote books for money without caring that they were full of mistakes. In any case, the Pope definitely heard about Buddhism from sources that did not know anything about it.

Buddhist teachings are infinite, since the revelations of the omniscient Buddha are infinite, reflecting the countless different faculties of beings through countless ways of connecting to them with skillful means and wisdom. These teachings can be categorized within the three levels of the vehicles[2] of the Hinayana,[3] Mahayana,[4] and Vajrayana.[5] But according to what the Pope has written, it seems that he has had just a little bit of exposure to only the Hinayana vehicle, as though he has scooped a few drops of water from an immeasurable ocean with a piece of grass and even misunderstood these few drops.

Without studying and understanding other doctrines deeply, to say many things about them is not wise. In particular, it is not enough just to say a few negative words, since it can create the tracks of hatred between religions, which is harmful to everyone. Whatever is said regarding the religious beliefs of millions of people should be considered in a vast way, said carefully, and proven in detail. One should make one's position clear, without distorting or adding one's own interpolations to the position of others. Instead, the Pope has first misrepresented Buddhist beliefs and then criticized them illogically.

1

EXPERIENCE AND ENLIGHTENMENT

The Pope writes,

> The enlightenment experienced by Buddha comes down to the conviction that the world is bad, that it is the source of evil and of suffering for man. [p. 85]

According to the Buddhist point of view, the enlightenment of Buddha cannot be described since it is beyond the understanding of ordinary mind. Although enlightenment is actually inexpressible in words or thoughts, it can be said for the benefit of sentient beings as an indication of its immeasurable qualities that it is always positive, inconceivable, nondual wisdom. It is especially peculiar to hear it described by the Pope as a conviction about evil, suffering, and the badness of the world.

Also, it is not said in Buddhism that Buddha "experienced" enlightenment. Enlightenment is beyond experience. Experience occurs between the duality of subject and object, and there is no existence of subject or object in enlightenment. Experience comes from feeling, and feeling belongs to sentient beings, not to fully enlightened Buddhas. Enlightenment is completely beyond either feeling or numbness.

From the point of view of the causal vehicle,[1] it can be said that Bodhisattvas,[2] sublime beings who are on the path of enlightenment and have not yet attained Buddhahood, still have experience due to traces of the residue of previous habit. Therefore, it could be said that when Buddha took birth many times as a Bodhisattva before attaining enlightenment, he had experience, including the experience of suffering caused by the passions,[3] which he later taught about when he attained the omniscience of fully enlightened Buddhahood. But this explanation of experience can be made only from the point of view of the causal vehicle, in which Bodhisattvas are differentiated from Buddhas. According to the resultant vehicle,[4] Bodhisattvas are fully enlightened manifestations of Buddhas effortlessly emanating for the benefit of beings and so they are also beyond experience, indivisible from the wisdom mind of Buddhas.

According to the Buddhist point of view, experience is always connected with dualistic mind. Dualistic mind depends on the ordinary inner elements[5] of sentient beings and ordinary outer elements of the substantial world, which are the basis of all that exists in duality. These ordinary elements are affected by inner root circumstances,[6] such as the conceptions of dualistic mind, and outer contributing circumstances,[7] such as the conditions of the substantial world, which always rely on each other and always change. The experience of sentient beings is to continually react to the circle of manipulation between subject and object, inner and outer elements, and root and contributing circumstances, which all continuously change because they are occupied by the habit of duality. The object is unreliable because the subject is unreliable, like a mental patient who depends on a schizophrenic psychiatrist. Sometimes he may feel worse and sometimes better, but he cannot transcend his situation because of endlessly circling between the subjective problems of the self and the objective problems of the other.

In duality, there is unceasing, meaningless movement back and forth between negative and positive feeling and experience. If negative circumstances arise, one says, "I feel unhappy," and if positive circumstances arise, one says, "I feel happy," just as the reflection of a body moves when a mirror moves, and the reflection in a mirror moves when the body moves. Instead of being locked in duality by constantly recreating it, Buddhist practitioners try to transform negative feeling and experience into positive feeling and experience through practice. This development of positive experience, which belongs to the path of enlightenment, is different from ordinary experience because experience is being transformed by the expansiveness of wisdom until the sublime state of Buddhahood is attained, which is beyond experience and feeling.

According to the Hinayana, all worldly experience, including positive experience, is only momentary and will change, and therefore causes suffering. Because they recognize this, the followers of the Hinayana develop detachment from external phenomena through prayer and meditation in order to attain nirvana.[8] Through their practice, they can find the ultimate cessation of the unreliable and senseless feeling and experience of suffering that comes from going back and forth between unhappiness and happiness.

According to the Mahayana, the followers of the Bodhisattva path practice to experience all phenomena as magic. Phenomena exist, but by seeing that their essence is empty, they do not cling to phenomena as real. At the same time, because the appearance of phenomena is unobstructed, there is not only inert nothingness, and phenomena can be used to accumulate virtue both substantially and nonsubstantially, with faith and love. Unhappiness and happiness are experienced as the same, equally substanceless magic, and all reality habit is understood to be a hallucination fabricated by dualistic mind, which is purified in nondual wisdom. Through immense love and faith, all experience on the path to enlightenment becomes positive. With effortless, undeliberated compassion and love for all sentient beings, including those who are less fortunate, followers can help sentient beings directly and indirectly. With immeasurable faith in flawless, fully enlightened Buddhas and sublime beings, they can see them and receive the experience of their blessings. In this way, Mahayana practitioners pray and pray, worship and worship, accumulate merit, and meditate until attaining full enlightenment, the same as Buddhas, beyond ordinary reality experience or unreal magic experience.

According to the Vajrayana, in order to attain wisdom body and its pure phenomena, followers receive sublime instructions from a wisdom teacher and, through practice, experience the transformation of ordinary body, speech, and mind and all existent phenomena into wisdom body, speech, mind, qualities, and activities through wisdom. Since the subject sees all existence as wisdom deity, all immeasurable objects are naturally seen as the pure phenomena of the Buddhas. Vajrayana practitioners do not try to be detached from this world or to see the phenomena of this world as magic but just believe and abide in wisdom and the purelands of the Buddhas. In this way, the transformation of all appearances automatically occurs. Even if practitioners are momentarily not capable of seeing in this way, it is due only to lack of faith and the residue of the previous habit of disbelief in pure deity phenomena, and these can change. They believe that all existence, including this universe, is pure because the subject is actually one's own original mind, and one's own original mind is wisdom. Since wisdom is pure, whatever manifests objectively or subjectively must be pure. From the perspective of the path of enlightenment, the Vajrayana has many profound teachings and methods to help others, with the skillful means of how to see and how to always have positive wisdom energy until attaining fully enlightened wisdom Buddhahood.

There is no question that whoever practices the Vajrayana to attain enlightenment in this life can help many beings, including those who are sick or have mental problems. But unfortunately, in this degenerate age, many Vajrayana practitioners are actually nihilists in disguise, not believing in Buddhas or deities and not having faith because they are afraid of losing their ordinary ego. They study Buddhism expecting the instant gratification of supporting their ordinary ego with the addition of knowledge, culture, or prestige, without faith, devotion, or belief, so they do not accomplish anything. It can be seen that their energy does not have anything special about it and that it only shows the signs of ordinary ego's vibration. They misuse what they study because they are only interested in material answers, trying to extract what they can for their own interests without having the capacity to acquire the confidence of being able to help other beings for their ultimate benefit. They have the idea that Buddhism is somehow useful for tricking other people in order to make their own life better. This problem of nihilism is often seen among Westerners who have become interested in Buddhism, but who like to find new subjects of research and experiments using new methods, and who try to force Buddhist ideas into their fixed, material conceptions. In spiritual traditions, one is supposed to rely not on material conceptions but on immaterial wisdom. But since they are actually nihilists, they become frustrated that there are so many categories and orders of teaching in Buddhism that are difficult for them to understand and to use because of their lack of having faith, practicing, and studying in a correct way. They make a mess by misusing Buddhism and then give the excuse that Buddhism does not deliver results for humankind. Instead of criticizing Buddhism from the vantage of nihilist habit, these people need to acknowledge their own lack of faith and spiritual qualities and begin to develop them.

2

EVIL, GOOD, AND REALITY

When the Pope says that the enlightenment of Buddha comes from a conviction that the world is bad and the source of evil and suffering (p. 85), he implies that evil and suffering are considered to exist in reality, and in a real world, particularly by Buddha. However, Buddha never taught that this world is only evil, or that the world's beings are objectively evil. Since he is fully enlightened, he does not have a conception of evil, so there is nothing that can cause evil.

According to the teachings of Buddhism, the source of evil is not the world. The source of evil is dualistic mind, or the grasping ego of mind, and the world is only a reflection of one's mind. It should be understood that in Buddhist teachings, without creating intellectual contradiction, a distinction is made between the wisdom mind of Buddha and the dualistic minds of sentient beings who have not yet attained enlightenment. According to the wisdom mind of Buddha, there is no evil, and according to the dualistic minds of sentient beings, the idea of evil must be purified.

From the Buddhist point of view, it is a misunderstanding to refer to the world as having an actual, material badness.

This misunderstanding seems to reflect the Pope's own idea that evil seriously exists somewhere externally or unchangeably, with clothes or naked, or with horns and a tail on a human being's body, or with a male upper body having a hairy chest, long mustache, and beard, and a female lower body. However, the Pope says that it is Buddhists who see the world as bad, and then he tries to show that this is a negative point of view. He writes,

> The Buddhist doctrine of salvation constitutes the central point, or rather the only point, of this system. Nevertheless, both the Buddhist tradition and the methods deriving from it have an almost exclusively negative soteriology. [p. 85]

This misunderstanding is the basis of the Pope's criticism in trying to establish that the

> doctrines of salvation in Buddhism and Christianity are opposed. [p. 85]

Of course, there are differences between the Christian and Buddhist doctrines of salvation. For example, Christianity is concerned with the salvation of humankind and not of other beings. Although Christianity teaches that one should have mercy toward animals, it also generally condones that animals can be used for the benefit of man under any circumstances for whatever he wishes. Buddhism teaches that one should have compassion for all immeasurable sentient beings, and that all sentient beings must be respected because they each hold the potential to attain Buddhahood. Salvation in Buddhism is meant for all sentient beings.

The Pope contrasts a theme of negativity and a view of the world as evil in Buddhism with the "positive approach" (p. 88) of Western civilization, and "positive attitude" (p. 88) inspired by Christianity. Referring to the Christian view as discussed in *Gaudium et Spes*, the Pope writes,

> These words indicate how between Christianity and the religions of the Far East, in particular Buddhism, there is an essentially different way of perceiving the world. . . . For Christianity, it does not make sense to speak of the world as a "radical" evil. [p. 89]

The Pope tries to compare Christian mysticism to Buddhism by saying that it is not negative because

> it is not born of an awareness of evil which exists in man's attachment to the world. [p. 87]

Yet although the Pope describes his idea of the Buddhist point of view as negative in the chapter on Buddhism, he describes the same point of view that he criticizes in Buddhism as a Christian view in other chapters. For example, while he presents Buddhism as having a "negative soteriology" (p. 85), he presents the Christian view that

> to save means to liberate from evil. [p. 69]

Of course, evil and suffering as they are perceived by ordinary beings with dualistic mind are considered in Buddhism and in all religions, but evil and suffering are obviously not related to enlightenment itself, which is the complete termination of evil and suffering. To observe the suffering of the ordinary world of dualistic perception is one of the teachings of the Hinayana that turns the mind toward Dharma,[1] but this teaching is actually given to recognize the nature of suffering so that the individual practitioner can abstain from suffering. The Hinayana view is to look at the suffering of the world, which is in the world and not in heaven, in order to become detached from it. This means that if one clings to the world of ordinary existence, then through attachment, one cannot liberate oneself from it to the peace that is beyond suffering. The example of suffering is used to teach how to be freed from suffering. That does not mean that evil and suffering in the world are considered to be real and that the world has to be attacked with weapons. There has never been even one word taught in Buddhism about the source of evil being in the world. Also, Buddhism has never advocated attacking anyone in the world.

As long as beings have the phenomena of suffering, Buddhism teaches that we must help them. That is why Buddha was reborn: to help beings. If something wrong were seen that could not be made right, that would be negative; but that is the opposite of Buddhism. Buddhism teaches that we must change what is wrong. If ordinary beings did not see something wrong in the world, then why did Jesus come to help? For what other reason could he have come?

The Buddhist perspective is that whatever is considered to be bad in the world comes from the deluded minds of sentient beings who created it from their own habits. So therefore, Buddhism teaches that one can stop the continuous suffering of this delusion, since each being has the potential to recognize the cause and result of suffering and then transform this suffering into happiness and peace.

My understanding of the Lord's Prayer, to "Our Father, who art in heaven," is that people are calling to God in order to make something good from what is bad, with the implication that there is indeed something bad or wrong in this world. Although the Pope claims that Buddhists consider the world to be bad, this actually seems to describe the words of this prayer, which ask God to "deliver us from evil." Surely this evil is found in the world and not heaven. That is why Christians pray "Thy kingdom come"—in order for evil to be eradicated and the qualities of heaven to manifest. That means that for now, anyway, this negativity or evil is considered to be on the earth, and that is why it is wished and prayed for the kingdom of God to come to earth, and for earth to become like heaven. The Pope seems to be like an innocent child who has lost his toy and is desperately and intensely staring into the dark to try to find it in each corner and each hallway with a flashlight, in the way that he is desperately and intensely searching for something to criticize about Buddhism, not noticing that his criticisms would apply to his own religion.

Christianity, including Catholicism, and all religions have the idea of sin. If sin means something bad, to me that means it has the same taste as evil, though maybe the shape is different, because both evil and sin cause suffering. If nothing bad is seen in the world, where does sin come from?

Also, the doctrines of both Christianity and Buddhism deal with the question of evil. If evil were not perceived in the world, then all religions, including Catholicism, would not need to build churches and teach about heaven, because there would be no need to change anything about this world and therefore there would be no need to have any conception of anything beyond this world. If religions teach about heaven, it means there is something wrong in the world according to the perception of sentient beings, including humankind. Since religions even talk about hell, which is worse, why can evil in the world not be discussed? It is better than hell. What is the purpose of teaching if the Pope believes the world is already good? Teachings are given in order to change. If the Pope prefers to teach about heaven, he can find that Buddhism also teaches about this.

Although Buddhism acknowledges that beings with deluded, dualistic perception have the phenomena of suffering, which includes the perception of evil, it does not call the world evil. Evil is not seen as an external monster. The way in which evil is understood depends on the perspectives of the different vehicles in Buddhism.

The Hinayana vehicle teaches that attachment is the source

of evil, and that attachment comes from ego. In order to be released from attachment, one must see the suffering of existence that is caused by each individual's attachment through the interdependent links[2] of relative truth[3] that occur between subject and object. According to the Hinayana, detachment is to unlink from circling between these links and to be free from one's own attachment. There are individual practices to accomplish this that purify the ego, exhaust the passions and karma,[4] and liberate oneself in the peace of nirvana. That does not mean that one sees a reality world of evil but that one should try to realize I-lessness by purifying the individual ego, in order to be released from the interdependent links of general and personal phenomena[5] that result in samsara.[6]

According to the Mahayana, all existence, including the existence of this world, is seen as magical, but beings who do not understand this create passions, karma, and suffering by believing it is real. The Mahayana teaches practitioners to help all beings who have this habit of reality through the activity of Bodhicitta[7] and the six paramitas.[8] That does not mean thinking the world is evil. In the Mahayana tradition, one's compassion for other beings increases by seeing that they have the conception that evil truly exists, increasing the wish to liberate them from their mind's creations of evil. Evil is not left as evil. Since evil is not concretized, it becomes that which is to be purified. Whatever is perceived as evil can be changed.

In the Vajrayana, all existence, including the existence of this world, can be recognized and sustained as totally pure phenomena through many different methods of opening to the wisdom appearances of deities and purelands inseparable with emptiness. That also does not mean thinking the world is evil. The Vajrayana teaches about primordially pure, luminous, unobstructedly compassionate wisdom deities. But this is not the time to talk about the Vajrayana. Christians may think Buddhist deities are evil since they are taught that sublime beings of other religions are false gods. So since whatever is seen depends on the individual's negative or positive reflection, which comes from the strength of their previous habit, some may see evil and some may see deity.

Although the Pope attempts to attach an idea of evil to Buddhism, it has never been taught in Buddhism that evil has any ultimate existence. The Pope mentions, however, the Christian idea of eternal damnation in his book (p. 73). I request with clasped hands that beings who are considered condemned to the hopeless idea of a permanent or eternal hell can cross the threshold of hope to go to heaven. In Buddhism, it is taught in the Mahayana and Vajrayana that even sinful beings can suddenly be enlightened if they have faith. According to the Vajrayana view of the Great Perfection teachings, not only is there no ultimate negativity or evil, but all existence is liberated from the beginning in the always noble, always greatest ecstasy. This must only be recognized and sustained through great faith and the blessing of sublime beings.

I have heard many times that through seeing paintings and statues of wrathful and peaceful Buddhas, many extremist Christians have thought, because of their reality orientation, that these paintings and statues were symbolic of devils, particularly unfamiliar wrathful aspects, causing them to get goose bumps from their own paranoia. They do not understand that these Buddhas, victorious over all evil conception, are the display of wisdom mind, in which there is nothing that can be harmed. Since these paintings and statues show only beneficial qualities, it is strange for Buddhists to hear that these same people who think different signs and expressions of Buddhas are terrible or feel seriously threatened by them, as though they were real to them, do not think hellish holy wars between religions are terrible, threatening, or even surprising, even though they occur in front of millions of people's eyes with actual fighting, killing, and suffering in a real way. It seems that they do not think of them as real, as though they visualized them, or they did not think of them as strange, as though they were the wrath of God.

If Christians have fear when they see bone ornaments, such as skulls filled with blood that symbolize emptying all suffering, and other aspects of wrathful deities such as weapons, which are signs of cutting all evil according to the Vajrayana tradition, how can they have faith in Jesus, who is depicted as terribly crucified and dripping with blood? If they think that this symbolizes his acceptance of crucifixion in order to take away the sins of others, what is the difference between this and wrathful deities who symbolize the purification of evil? Buddhists are not afraid when they see Jesus on the cross, and they do not have goose bumps, because they know it is a sign of something special. They are not going to think that there is anything negative about Jesus or be terrified to see or hear that Jesus was crucified and resurrected. Since Buddhists believe that spiritual appearances occur according to the phenomena of beings, they can accept that this can exist even though it is unfamiliar to them. They can consider it a positive history of a sublime being who benefits other beings, and just leave it as it is.

According to the Mahayana tradition, it can be said that even different appearances of God and forms of God can be manifested from Buddhas and can be manifestations of Buddhas, so whoever truly understands the Mahayana teachings about the manifestations of Buddhas, which occur according to the different phenomena of sentient beings, will not think that Jesus is evil, attack him, insult him, or call his religion "purely negative" (p. 87).

The Buddhist understanding of evil is very different than the Pope's identification of evil as a definite reality. In Buddhism, even if evil seems to exist in both the outer world of general phenomena, which is shared by individuals, and the inner world of personal phenomena, which is within the personal creations of an individual, evil is always caused by grasping mind. Many other religions think that evil exists independently of the mind. Buddhism teaches that even though evil seems to exist independently, it is still only created by the habit of one's mind and has no inherent existence.

Buddha Shakyamuni is fully enlightened beyond conceptions of evil. But in order for sentient beings to recognize the non-evil mind of Buddhahood, he introduced the way evil is created by the delusions of sentient beings and showed how to annihilate the source of evil. Since Buddha is omniscient, he can describe anything. Buddha defined four kinds of evil for the benefit of sentient beings who still have the phenomena of evil, so they can be released from their reality projections of evil by understanding how they are creating them.

The evil of the passions is caused when the mind grasps and rejects its creations of desirable and aversive phenomena. The ego causes passions.

The passions cause reality form, which causes suffering. Beings suffer because of substance, since whenever there is reality form, one has to take care of it. This is *the evil of the skandhas*[9] of grasping ego.

Whatever is formed within the substance of the ordinary five skandhas must again diminish and die. This is *the evil that robs life*.

Anything that causes attachment to desirable qualities, such as power, fame, and possessions, lures beings through its seductiveness and causes obstacles that do not let beings become free from suffering. This is *the evil of the gods*, which is always to hope for and want to find these desirable qualities. It should not be misinterpreted that this concerns the formless gods of other religions, since this occurs within form. It is called this because it comes from the wish for attachment. Although it may not seem to be negative, it inevitably causes suffering because it does not last. There is nothing that can be permanent unless it causes enlightenment. Attachment prevents enlightenment by drawing one toward the objects of attraction.

Buddha taught that all of these kinds of evil can cease through one's own mind. In order for the source of evil to cease, the source must be recognized as one's negative conception. Buddha showed at the Hinayana level that negative conceptions come from the grasping of the ego. If the ego is purified by practice and realization, dualistic mind is reduced and therefore grasping and the passions are reduced, so karma is reduced. Whenever karma ceases, so that all negative phenomena have ceased, it is called nirvana.

There was once a Zen master who was asked by a samurai warrior to teach him the meaning of hell and heaven. When the master answered, "I will never teach anything to anyone as violent and idiotic as you," the samurai became very angry, raised his sword, and was about to stab the master. The master said to him, "That is hell." Immediately, the samurai understood, threw down his sword in recognition, and bowed to the master with faith. Then the master said, "That is heaven." Buddhists believe that there is hell and heaven unless they purify their dualistic negative habit into positive habit through practicing and go from positive habit to no habit, which is fully enlightened, stainless Buddhahood. Hell is created by the habit of negative conception and its projection, and heaven is created by positive phenomena. If one plants a bean, the result is not going to be a rice plant; if the seed is rice, the result must be rice. So until dualistic mind's habit is exhausted into fully enlightened Buddhahood, Buddhists try not to cause the sediment of habits that create hell and try instead to develop and increase virtue in order to attain fully enlightened Buddhahood. All are from mind. That is why Shantideva, the Indian Buddhist scholar of ancient times, said,

The phenomena of hell are caused by sin. Other than that, there is no hell that exists independently. When-

ever one's own dualistic negative habit of sin is purified, there is no personal phenomenon of hell.

Evil does not come from somewhere outside oneself, so
that one should try to get rid of it outwardly. It is given its existence inwardly, by falling in love with evil. Buddhists realize
that it is negative conceptions that are evil. If one does not
change the grasping of evil through one's own mind, it causes
one to see evil in the external world.

When the Tibetan saint Milarepa found his retreat cave
occupied by a rock spirit, he was afraid and tried to exorcise
her. Then the rock spirit answered with this song:

If the conception of an enemy does not arise
As a consequence of one's own deluded mind,
For what reason do I, a rock spirit, become your enemy?
In general, this demon of habit comes from one's own
    deluded mind.
If you do not realize your own mind is emptiness,
There are many other demons besides me.
If you realize the nature of your own mind,
All bad circumstances become good friends.
Even I, a rock spirit, will also be your servant.

Milarepa remembered his teacher, who had introduced
that all phenomena come from one's own mind, one's own
mind is emptiness, and emptiness is Dharmakaya.[10] He encour-
aged himself with these words, gave up outward exorcism, and
stayed in his cave without fear. The rock spirit disappeared.

From the text called *Cutting Ego,* in *The Song of Laughing
Dakinis* by the great Vidyadhara Fearless Islander, it is said:

Sustaining in the fearless path of enlightenment, I, a yogi,
With the point of view that the activity of samsara and
    nirvana are equal,

Dance on the demons and gods of grasping mind.
The evil of dualistic mind is crushed into dust.

With this level of accomplishment, samsara and nirvana are equally pure.

According to the Mahayana, it is possible to rekindle dormant Buddha nature through realizing that it is inherent in one's own mind, believing in Buddha with faith, and then purifying the negative, dualistic habit of one's own mind. The existence of evil cannot be reduced unless our own evil is reduced. The habit of the perception of evil is reduced by prayer and meditation, and one's mind becomes more pure. Then through the reflection of this subjective purification, the heavy elements of objective existence become lighter and more pure, expanding more and more. Through the interdependence of circumstances, as much as attachment is reduced, compassion grows, and as much as the conception of evil is reduced, it is naturally transformed into love. As Buddha phenomena increase, the purity of all existence can be seen from the indivisible state.

If evil is just left as evil, man is left as man, God is left as God, and love is left as love, then it is very hard for there to be any vast benefit because everything has already been made into something fragmented and static. Whatever has already been made into something builds more belief in its reality, so we build something that is already there into something more. It becomes like forever having to deal with technical equipment. If one piece of the equipment is missing, the rest will not function, so one always needs to pay attention to having all pieces of the equipment, and one becomes fixed and trapped in it. Then one cannot find the freedom of wisdom. Spiritual liberation does not cause this fragmented collection of conceptions.

The Pope says that Buddhists

do not free [them]selves from evil through the good which comes from God. [p. 86]

Buddhists do not liberate themselves and others by the goodness of God but by the goodness of Buddha. Buddhists believe
that both what is bad and what is good come from karma.
They pray to Buddha for bad not to come and for good to
come, and they accumulate merit in order for good to come.
There is really nothing wrong if they do not pray to the same
God that the Pope recognizes. But according to the Pope, one
must believe in God and Jesus, and other beliefs are unaccept-
able. Since the Pope seems to think Buddhism is bad because he
thinks Buddhists should have a different God, it looks as
though he would also not want Buddhists to be practicing and
meditating according to their beliefs. This would cause them to
be distanced from their spiritual goal by not uniting with Buddha. It seems that the Pope would rather prevent others from
following their own beliefs and religion, if they are different
from his, instead of just encouraging spirituality.

When the Pope talks about good that comes from God,
does he mean material good or spiritual good? If he is referring to material goodness, then how is it explained that some
nihilists still have good material circumstances without having prayed to God for one second? Buddhism teaches that
even if one does not pray in this life, goodness comes from the
karmic result of prayers made in previous lives, so the effect of
praying cannot be evaluated only in a material way by what
can be observed. Also, some people from different religions
who pray to one God are continuously fighting with each
other. Good and love should come from sublime beings, not
fighting. If the Pope is referring to spiritual good that comes
from God, why does he talk so much about evil? That does
not seem good.

Buddhists think bad and good are just interdependent circumstances which are created by dualistic habit. It does not
mean they believe in the reality of some evil form, such as an
evil world, but that reality thinking is evil. What seems to be
bad comes from habit, a lack of faith in Buddha and one's own

Buddha nature, and a lack of practicing to attain enlighten-ment. Since evil and good exist until dualistic mind is purified, Buddhists believe that we should recognize Buddha nature to achieve fully enlightened Buddhahood, for the benefit of all beings attaining unfathomable Buddhahood.

Therefore, it is a mistake for the Pope to say that Buddhism is a "negative soteriology" (p. 85) based on detachment from evil, since Buddhism is based on how to create and attain the positive energy of the inconceivable purity of the unending union of space and appearance, which is the infallibility of Buddhahood. If the Pope is critical of the idea of the world as evil, then he should know about the Mahayana doctrine of Buddhism, which teaches that all phenomena are magic and do not cause an object of grasping, but that phenomena can still be used for creating merit through good habit until attaining fully enlightened Buddhahood, beyond reality or magic. If the Pope does not want to think of the world as negative, then he should know about the Vajrayana doctrine, which teaches to transform phenomena into pure, positive appearances.

3

BREAKING TIES TO REALITY

The Pope thinks that Buddhists believe that

> to liberate oneself from evil, one must free oneself from this world, necessitating a break with the ties that join us to external reality—ties existing in our human nature, in our psyche, in our bodies. The more we are liberated from these ties, the more we become indifferent to what is in the world, and the more we are freed from suffering, from the evil that has its source in the world. [pp. 85–86]

These words clearly show that the Pope misunderstands the Buddhist view of reality and the external world. Even the Pope's definition of what constitutes the world differs immensely from the Buddhist view. Although the Pope does not mention the names of Europe, Asia, Africa, Australia, and the Americas, he seems to believe strongly that the world consists of only the continents of this earth and its human inhabitants. According to Buddhism, innumerable worlds make up all immeasurable existence, including this particular world of sentient beings as well as countless other realms and beings.

In Buddhism, the characteristics of the world depend on the general and personal phenomena of time and place. The world is not always positive and not always negative because it is created by and is the consequence of karma. As long as the habit of dualistic mind exists, the aspect in which the world appears always changes individually and generally according to the changing conceptions of beings. Buddhism teaches that whatever changes is not the unchangeable, everlasting state, which is Buddhahood. Whether the world seems temporarily negative or positive, it will not remain that way but will perpetually change. The only unchanging, everlasting peace is fully enlightened Buddhahood, which can be reached through prayer, faith, and meditation.

The Pope mentions only the world of humankind, or the human realm, and not other realms of sentient beings, but even just considering the reality of the realm of humankind, one can see that it cannot be permanent and has particular kinds of suffering. Taking birth is a form of suffering. After birth, there is so much suffering for infants. They cannot talk or do anything independently and are full of frustration over their powerlessness. Then when people get old, they do not want to abandon youthful circumstances, reminiscing about their past although they cannot make the situations of their youth happen again in the same way. Their young energy decreases like a flower fading from a drought, and they do not have the same strength as before, whether they are poor or rich. They are naturally dismissed from society, like an animal isolated from a flock, and are often ignored by young people. This causes a lot of suffering. Then without question, whoever has a body will get sick, and there is so much worry about how to cure illness. Finally, when death comes, people are always afraid to die unless they are good meditators. Even while they are living, people are always suffering, always concerned about who will be an enemy and harass them, and about loved ones and having to separate from them. What is wished may not succeed, and what is not wished, such as different kinds of disasters, may come. There is obvious, undeniable suffering for human beings, even though the human realm is better than other realms. So practitioners of the Hinayana tradition think that wherever one is born, there will be suffering, and with aversion for this suffering, they become detached. This detachment is not from other beings but is being detached themselves. It does not mean staying in some kind of dullness, but studying, praying to Buddha, receiving blessings, and meditating to attain nirvana, the state of Arhat.[1]

As dualistic mind is reduced through practice, there are fewer and fewer reality phenomena until duality is exhausted. Also, through practice, when nondualistic wisdom mind is realized through meditation, one can see that everything is interdependent, and one can realize the nonessence of reality. This can be decided when dualistic mind is exhausted in wisdom.

Buddhists do not believe it is important to maintain a connection to ordinary, external reality, as the Pope does (pp. 88–89). Yet Buddhism has never taught that to be liberated from evil, one must break one's ties to the external reality of the world, as the Pope claims. Buddhism does not focus on external reality but on the development of inner spirituality. Of course, Buddhist practitioners have to depend on external circumstances of interdependent phenomena as long as they still have these phenomena due to their residual karma. Their aim, however, is to purify dualistic mind, which is the source of interdependent phenomena, to the state of nondependent enlightenment, the same as Buddha. This is very different from excessive preoccupation with external reality. This preoccupation, even though it may seem to be related to spirituality, can signify adherence to a nihilist view of turning only to that reality, which is actual atheism, and away from the essence of appearances, which is free from destructibility. As the Pope knows, there are some people who talk about spirituality but do not have faith, using the language of spirituality in a material context and using religion as though it were a business. They do this because they are centered on their interests in external reality rather than engaged in actual spirituality.

Whatever the Pope discusses about Buddhism is within the context of reality, about reality men in a reality world. In spiritual terms, one can talk about what is real or unreal and their inextricable relation to each other, in order to recognize that it is only dualistic conception to think something is real or unreal. Otherwise, it is unnecessary for me and the Pope to go back and forth between what is real and unreal. Whoever wants to keep reality phenomena can have reality, and whoever wants to keep unreality phenomena can have unreality, like magic. Also, whoever wants to keep the point of view of the indivisibility of reality and unreality can do so. Reality and unreality are just conceptions within interdependent relative truth. We think something is real when we are dreaming, and when we awaken, we think it is unreal. But neither is any more real than the other if we can recognize that they are both the fabrications of the mind. For example, if a barren woman dreams her baby has died, thinking it is real, that is conception. When she recognizes as she awakens that she has no baby, thinking it is unreal, that is also just conception.

Even when giving up the world is mentioned in some Buddhist teachings, it does not mean that the world is seen as objectively real or evil. It means that remaining in dualistic habit causes evil phenomena that come from one's own mind. Likewise, when it is sometimes said that the world must be emptied, this does not mean to kill anyone. It means that one should decimate one's own hatred, attachment, and negative habit, which is the purification of one's own evil and does not cause problems for anyone. This is great love. According to the Hinayana, one's own passions are the enemy of the path of enlightenment, so one has to annihilate them through meditation. Since ego is the source of the passions, one does this by purifying the ego. The Pope does not need to worry that the detachment of Hinayana practitioners will empty the world of phenomena, since they do not have an idea that the world will disappear according to general phenomena.

This does not mean that they intentionally reject or break away from the world, as the Pope implies; they just leave it as it is. According to the Hinayana, the world is not denied or harmed when the cessation of suffering and the attainment of peace occurs for each individual through prayer and meditation, with or without a group. Surely the Pope accepts the benefit of individual spiritual attainment without insisting on seeing some obvious, substantial benefit from one man to another that always involves their visible human bodies and activities between these substantial bodies. That is not a spiritual perspective.

When dualistic mind individually ceases, the one for whom it ceases does not have the phenomena of sentient beings, because nirvana has been attained. This must be explained here since it is unlike the Pope's version of the Hinayana, which gives the impression that when the phenomena of nirvana, sentient beings must still remain in front of one. In the state of nirvana, even though reality phenomena have ceased according to individual phenomena, reality still exists according to general phenomena—going, coming, diminishing, and increasing through beings' habits. But these reality phenomena are considered to be impermanent and cause more weariness for this world.

In Buddhism, it is taught that when the grasping phenomena of the circle of ordinary existence cease, there is no conception of other beings and there is no conception of the world. If one is actually liberated oneself, there is no conception that one has gone somewhere else away from others who are left behind in a reality world. When dualistic habit ceases, which is the state of enlightenment, there is no conception of either self or other.

Although the Pope disapproves of giving up the external world, freeing oneself from suffering by spiritual practice is at least not bad, since it is not fighting with guns and weapons, killing many hundreds and thousands of people as those in some other religions do. It is much better to purify one's passions and liberate oneself by practice than to look only toward the external world, causing conflicts with others that endure for many generations and perpetuating what is impossible to finish by remaining enmeshed in the passions.

Even though the Pope has misrepresented the Buddhist view of detachment, he should compare his version of detachment to retribution as it is presented by Christians on television who caution viewers that if they do something wrong, they will be punished by God. It is often said by Christians that bad circumstances in the external world mean that God is punishing people. If the personal detachment of individuals is considered to be bad, what about the world becoming bad from God's punishment? That is worse than detachment. That is not compassion. Real punishment in the external world is worse than personal detachment.

Buddhists believe that bad circumstances in the external world are the karmic result of the previous bad deeds of sentient beings. Buddhists do not believe that it is divine punishment if something bad happens; they believe that one should never blame the results of one's own bad deeds on Buddha or God. According to Buddhists, it is better to acknowledge one's karma and then try to change bad karma into good karma through faith in Buddha and God and love toward beings, in order to create and accumulate merit. Making this choice depends only on the intention of each individual. If one faces a mirror with a grimace, the reflection of a grimace returns. If one faces a mirror with a joyful expression, a reflection of joy returns. I myself only want to believe in the blessings of Buddhas and God to beings because that is the pure nature of Buddhas and God.

The Pope writes that ties to external reality exist in human nature, the psyche, and the body, but I do not understand how this could be so. In defining his view of Buddhism, the Pope says these ties to external reality must be broken, but in his view of Christianity, these ties do not need to be broken. Actually, whether individual Buddhists can break their attachment to external reality depends on their wishes and capacities. This is the same as it is for individuals in other religions. It cannot be said that Buddhists in general want to break ties to external reality. But actually, what is wrong with breaking these ties if it reduces and purifies negative defilements? It is not against anyone. Regarding Buddhism, the Pope writes,

> To indulge in a negative attitude toward the world in the conviction that it is only a source of suffering for man and that he therefore must break away from it, is negative not only because it is unilateral, but because it is fundamentally contrary to the development of both man himself and the world, which the Creator has given and entrusted to man as his task. [pp. 88–89]

This does not sound like it is being said at a spiritual level, since not to go beyond the world, but to think only of dealing with it, is closer to nonspiritual psychological ideas, which are involved only with the interests of this life, than to spiritual ideas, which are for the benefit of uniting with God. If an individual's ties to the world are too tight, or cannot be broken, there is no channel, exit, or open door for heaven to come to earth, or for earth to transform into heaven. The Pope should think in a vaster way than this, so that if it is necessary, ties to external reality can be broken so that heaven can come to earth and earth can transform into heaven, beyond one who breaks or what is broken, to benefit beings. The unilateral decision that one should not break away from the external world means that one is only concerned with living in this world and owning this world and is not remembering or considering heaven and God.

If one is supposed not to break ties to the world, but to develop man and the world, there cannot be any long-term benefit for many beings to develop whatever capacity they have to abstain from nonvirtue and create virtue, to be spiritual, to go to heaven, and to finally unite with God. Instead of spiritual development, a recommendation to develop man and the world sounds more like the idea of a nonreligious, competitive company trying to develop its profits. It is only thinking of this world, and not the ultimate "divinization of man" (p. 195), to stay within the confines of ordinary human nature, an indecisive psyche, a diminishable, fragile body, and a changeable world.

If these three ties were continuous as the Pope implies they should be, then heaven would become useless, since it would seem better not to pray to be reborn in heaven because one would have to keep these three ties. In my understanding, these three ties are not precious since they do not cause enlightenment but can cause the habit of being bound with a heavy chain. If one is bound instead of being liberated, how can one join with God? God does not have these three ties. If one forms a strong habit of keeping these three ties in this way, this habit can be retained for many lives. How can one then unite with God, who is tieless? If one does not ever break these ties, but keeps the conception of being tied, what is the benefit of praying to God and trying to unite with God? What is enlightenment? What does celestial mean, and what is heaven? When and how can one approach these? Should one just keep their names without paying attention to them, and give up trying to go there?

It is difficult to understand the logic of grouping human nature, the psyche, and the body together with the implication that one must always be tied to them because breaking away from them is negative. According to the Buddhist view, one cannot remain tied to them because they cannot always exist since the body changes, the psyche changes, and the nature of a being changes due to karma. Since they are changeable, these three ties cannot stay together in the same way forever and are naturally going to change, so breaking away from them is inevitable.

TIES TO HUMAN NATURE

According to Buddhism, human nature is variable, uncertain, and depends on previous karma. Differences in human nature are created by mind through intention, which is based on mind. In order to change negative natures to positive natures and to be released from circling between negative and positive, according to the point of view of the vehicle, Buddhists try to abstain from, purify, or transform what is bad into what is good through prayer, practice, and meditation. To be liberated from evil, one does not try to free oneself from the world. There is no need to try to concentrate on breaking ties to external reality, since not only one's nature but all reality and unreality are just reflections of the mind.

Unless one goes beyond karma through faith, devotion, and practice to attain fully enlightened Buddhahood, the attributes of human nature always depend on beings' habit. If there is bad habit, beings can be reborn with negative habit and energy in lower realms, and if there is good habit, beings can be reborn with positive habit and energy in higher realms. Beings cannot always have human nature. For example, if humans do bad things, human nature can change into animal nature, and similarly, through the result of previous good karma, animal nature can become human nature. Each individual who has not achieved full enlightenment can be born in the human realm or in other realms, and wherever they are born, they take the nature, as well as the body and psyche, of that realm of existence. All of these are impermanent, however, and have to continually change into different natures, bodies, and psyches when beings are reborn. As the Pope knows, the human body must be left someday, and according to Buddhism, whenever it is left, the mind has to follow after whatever habit was previously made. When that happens, the ties to a particular nature must also change. Even though beings may temporarily exist as humans, they have no power to always belong to humanity.

In Buddhist theory, human nature is characterized by the ability to talk, understand language, and communicate with other human beings, as well as the ability to tame wild animals and distinguish between what is wrong and right. Ordinary human nature at a worldly level is characterized by the wish to develop prestige, to be ambitious for one's own interests, and to build ego through one's qualities or position. All of these have to do with the passions and the ego and deal only with the external world. They do not involve thinking about previous lives, future lives, hell, or heaven but just involve trying to construct a reputation and its influence for this life. With this attitude, even when someone wants to help others, there is always an expectation of some substantial reward in return. Ordinary human nature is opportunistic, since it does not have the depth of spiritual qualities. Its worldly phenomena can be synthesized in these eight main categories: if one succeeds at whatever one wishes, one is happy; if one does not succeed at whatever one wishes, one is unhappy; if one has a comfortable life for oneself and one's side, one is happy; if one has an uncomfortable life for oneself and one's side, one is unhappy; if one has a good reputation, one is happy; if one has a bad reputation, one is unhappy; if one is praised by others, one is happy; and if one is insulted by others, one is unhappy.

Precious human nature at a level of spiritual wisdom is characterized by believing that even though one depends temporarily on the external world due to having been born in the world from previous karma, one's mind is not the same as in previous lives because it is becoming sublime. However sublime the mind becomes with spiritual wisdom, that much even the body changes through the influence of the mind until, through the accumulation of merit and wisdom, the fully enlightened state is achieved. With belief in an everlasting quality beyond this external world, one tries to find and develop this quality through cultivating one's own inner, positive spiritual qualities and by following in the footsteps of previous sublime beings through faith, deep devotion, prayer, and meditation, in order to help other beings both tangibly and intangibly. Even tangible positive qualities are created from intangible spiritual qualities. Whenever inner spiritual qualities progress, there is a much greater ability to benefit other beings profoundly and at all times, not only temporarily within a small part of substantial existence but also within infinite insubstantial phenomena. The characteristics of precious human nature are having faith in Buddha; having love for all sentient beings, not only one's family; being disciplined; and being able to meditate and become enlightened for the benefit of all sentient beings.

In the Buddhist tradition, one uses this precious human nature by trying to find good circumstances, such as having a good teacher and receiving teachings, so that faith and devotion can increase and wisdom energy can develop. This world or other realms of higher beings can be used to connect with positive circumstances for the purpose of joining root circumstances, such as Buddha nature, with contributing circumstances, such as teachings, to change one's mind. Through the interdependence of good circumstances, the mind can change from being ordinary to spiritual, and from being spiritual to sublime, to attain enlightenment. The world is not only the external world of this earth. One can join with the sublime beings of other realms, although nihilists do not accept this, for spiritual development. But that does not mean being tied to some external realm. Anything in existence can be used until spiritual power is perfectly accomplished. There is no need to worry about breaking or not breaking ties to the external world. Until bad circumstances change to good circumstances, and good circumstances change to sublime spiritual phenomena to achieve the enlightenment of Buddhafields, there will be continuous positive change, so it is unnecessary to be tied to some certain external world.

So of the two kinds of human natures just discussed, the Pope probably means ordinary human nature, which is connected to the passions, because it deals substantially only with this external world, since according to the Pope's advice, ties cannot be broken to the external world.

TIES TO THE PSYCHE

The psyche can mean either the mind or the soul, and I do not understand clearly which meaning the Pope intends. If the Pope is talking about the psyche in a spiritual way as it pertains to the soul, which is more vast, then it would be unnecessary to be afraid if the soul were to break with the external world. If he is thinking only of an ordinary, nonspiritual idea of the mind, perhaps the Pope means that the mind must be connected to whatever is seen and thought, so it cannot break with the world. But when only a nihilist point of view of the mind is considered in this way, it is very limited if one wants to help others, since one can only help a few complementary beings with a view that only relates to momentary substantial phenomena. Buddhists believe in the long-term spiritual benefit that comes from having faith in Buddha and praying to receive blessings to attain the flawless wisdom body of fully enlightened Buddhahood, which can help others within both substantial and insubstantial phenomena.

If the psyche is just left as it is, what is the benefit of God or any sublime beings, since what can be done if one is supposed to leave the mind and the world as they are? If the psyche stays attached to the world, it causes ego and distraction toward materialism through a lack of nondual wisdom. The psyche of ordinary human beings cannot be ultimately beneficial even psychologically. Although it may seem superficially positive, it will not be long lasting or vast. The ordinary psyche just causes more distraction toward the ordinary world, supporting a nihilist point of view that reduces incisiveness due to the limitation of materialism. With this narrowed view, beings cannot always see immediate results from spiritual qualities, so they do not value them or try to develop them. They do not realize that what is seen is uncertain because it depends on the one who is seeing, nor that spiritual qualities are not apparent to them due to their way of seeing. Then they just leave their ordinary psyche as it is, even though it cannot benefit them. Spiritual qualities are always beneficial because they are not occupied by solid dualistic habit but permeated by nondual wisdom. By developing the spiritual qualities of the mind, one can benefit others because one is not attached to this world. As much as one does not grasp strongly toward objects, one gives that much space to others to release their own grasping and recognize spiritual qualities.

It seems that the Pope does not want human nature, the psyche, and the body to be lost, since he thinks they are necessary as a basis for relating to God in this world. The Pope seems to think that the Hinayana practice to achieve egolessness involves a terrible loss of self, and he wants to be kind to man as he is without scaring him with a threat of losing himself. He seems to want to preserve man's sense of self because a self is needed to have a soul, which is the immortal part of man, and the soul is related to God. Therefore, the Pope implies that one has to continuously maintain a self, or ego, in order not to lose everything, including God. But according to the logic of the necessity of maintaining a self and the fear of selflessness, how can an impure, mortal humankind ever unite with a pure, immortal God?

Buddhists do not believe in the ultimate significance of an

ordinary soul or psyche, or in anything that must remain tied to dualistic habit; they believe in inconceivable wisdom. One is supposed to lose the impure phenomena of dualistic habit, such as a self, in order to gain the state of victory, which is union. Buddhists think that if there is a fear of losing one's self, or ordinary ego, then there is no connection with wisdom. Keeping the dualistic habit of separating humankind from God does not cause God. If one leaves humankind as it is, which is changeable and diminishable, through being tied to the psyche, and if one leaves God as indestructible and separated from humankind, then how, when, and in what place are man and God going to join in union? If God is sublime and one unites with God, that means one naturally transforms, separates, and releases from an ordinary psyche through the influence of wisdom.

Even if the psyche is defined as meaning the soul and one thinks that the human soul is immortal, it will automatically remain mortal if one does not want to lose ordinary ego. Then even though an immortal soul exists intangibly, it will not be transformed into actual immortality through its ability to open and join with a totally pure, immortal God because of being continuously occupied by duality, making the immortal soul static and leaving it dormant forever. Instead of suppressing it with the misinterpretation of mortality and immortality and always trying to maintain duality, why not believe in an immortal God and try to rekindle the intrinsic immortality of man? Why not let it blossom freely until it is totally united with a pure, immortal God, just worshipping and praying the Lord's Prayer, saying and believing it until becoming indivisible with God? What is wrong with that? Since God is immortal and always has inconceivable qualities manifesting with wisdom power, God cannot cease, even though God is called formless.

It is very tiring to say and think overtly that one's soul is immortal but to not deeply believe it, walking a dualistic path without letting go of dualistic ego and so at the same time remaining mortal. It is just like a weak traveler who aimlessly steps toward a targetless place, exhausting himself.

Ordinary people are afraid to lose their ego by thinking in a spiritual way. They worry that they will lose their own power if they surrender to Buddha or God, since they do not have a spiritual idea of uniting with Buddha or God. Religious eternalists are afraid if it is said that they have to be selfless because they think it means they will lose everything, including God and their psyche, or soul. Actually, to be selfless is not losing, but gaining, since by reducing dualistic habit, wisdom expands, and that is always powerful. That is triumphant.

According to Buddhism, all ordinary existence and all appearances of enlightenment come from one basic mind. One cannot show that this basic mind is white, green, square, round, or anything at all, but from this basic mind can arise any phenomena according to the choice of beings. As said by the saint Sarahapa:

> The sole, essential nature of mind is the source of all
>   phenomena.
> Wherever existence and enlightenment manifest,
> The fruit of whatever is wished is given.
> I bow to mind, which is the wish-fulfilling jewel.

In the Mahayana tradition, the immortal, spiritual essence of all sentient beings is called Buddha nature, according to basic mind. This means that this essence has not blossomed but is a dormant potential within dualistic mind. From the result of previous prayers, this root circumstance of Buddha nature cannot connect with contributing circumstances such as meeting a good teacher and accumulating merit so that Buddha nature can be rekindled. When inherent Buddha nature is realized and completely opened, all dualistic human nature and the psyche, which are occupied by dualistic habit, are finished, which is called fully enlightened Buddhahood. Then there is no separation between Buddha nature and Buddha. At that time, there is no idea of any ordinary psyche, intrinsic quality, or potential, because Buddha nature has already been rekindled and completely opened, so there is no ordinary psyche remaining, which is totally immortal enlightened Buddhahood, abiding inconceivably forever.

When the Pope talks about the psyche, if he is referring to the soul as the spiritual and immortal part of human beings, it is much more wonderful than the nihilist way of thinking that one only has this momentary life and then dies, since it is logically much more hopeful to believe that there can eventually be union with God. But at the time of union, one is supposed to leave the part that is human, so that when one is united with God, it becomes a union beyond a collection of separate parts. If ties to a soul must be kept, as well as to one's human nature and body, it is still a way of sustaining samsaric phenomena since it is engaged with gross substance. If human beings have to maintain a real human nature, it will always be occupied by dualistic habit and the passions of desire, jealousy, arrogance, hatred, and ignorance, as everyone knows, including even nihilists who do not have a spiritual level of understanding. Ordinary human senses decay, ordinary human feelings are impermanent, and ordinary human consciousness changes according to conception. There is nothing left that is particularly special about ordinary human nature. When the immortal, spiritual aspect of humans is not rekindled but just left mingling with ordinary human nature, its benefit is lost. To attain union with God, ordinary human nature must be purified, or the idea of union will just remain a mental abstraction. One cannot be liberated without transforming ordinary human nature. Even if the immortal aspect of human beings does not stop, ordinary human nature will vanish, since it continuously changes. If ordinary human nature and the spiritual aspect of human beings are always supposed to go together, as though they had been fixed in that way from the beginning with the decision that they must never be separated, it would be discouraging for the attainment of liberation. For me, this is very confusing, because if one tries to join with God, a connection cannot be made since it would appear to be criminal to give up human nature, and it would be breaking laws to break ties. So even though it is obviously true that one cannot keep ordinary human nature and also be liberated, the Pope insists on and imposes the idea that one still has to keep it. The Pope's idea is that God must be left as God, and one cannot liberate oneself in order to unite with God. One cannot touch, but just be close.

This is why Buddhism is so precious. It shows how to abide with Buddha phenomena, in which two things never exist, and how, through the power of the blessing and wisdom of the Buddhas, to become inseparable with the Buddhas in total liberation. However, saying this is too threatening for some people.

For me, God must be totally pure. Through prayer, devotion, and worship, one should try to abide with God when on the path of union with God, even though God is beyond imagination. Then ordinary human nature will be reduced and the immortal aspect of humans will expand, so that one becomes closer to God through meditation and faith. Someday, beyond becoming close, one can unite with God to be liberated. It is very hard to know when one can be liberated if an immortal soul is left with human nature, because it will not be able to expand beyond that human nature. If the immortal aspect of humans just has to be left mixed with human nature, it will not be enlivened. Instead of getting close to God, one will become more distant. The potential for union with God will just remain in the imagination, although I still respect the Pope's thought that he is dealing with the influence of spirituality. This is only my logic in response to what was written by the Pope, and I do not want to add to what is said in the Bible or to the way that people think. So the Pope can keep this human aspect, but if one has the conception of keeping one's humanity, it seems that hope is being lost. If one must always plan to keep oneself and God separate, how can a union occur? Even though one says the word of union, one has already decided that one does not want union when one thinks that one's soul is lost if the human aspect is lost.

In the Hinayana, it is taught that eons can pass before one achieves fully enlightened Buddhahood. The time involved depends on the individual's point of view and practice, but it is definite that liberation will ultimately occur, so there is hope. In the Mahayana, the root circumstance of Buddha nature, or one's potential to attain enlightenment, is already there and can connect with the contributing circumstances of prayers, practice, the accumulation of merit, and meditation. As the quality of Buddha nature increases, the idea of any human aspect becomes less. Even the idea of an intrinsic Buddha nature becomes less due to the power of the blessing of Buddha nature. When Buddhahood is reached, all conceptions of Buddha nature, root circumstances, or contributing circumstances vanish. There is nothing that can be divided since all has become indivisible oneness.

If faith is not developed and the immortal aspect of humans is left as it is, it becomes inactive and does not function. But by developing faith, one can link this immortal aspect with an immortal God until the hope of union eventually becomes an actual, immortal union. If the immortal aspect of humans is just thought of as immortal but not allowed to be actualized, it prevents union. This happens through the conception of needing to stay tied to the world without breaking away from it, because to do so would be, as mentioned before, "fundamentally contrary to the development of man and the world" (p. 88). If this idea were true, it would mean that salvation would not be allowed because of having to keep tied to the world. Man could not be saved because he would have to remain bound to his human nature, and human nature cannot cause salvation. Yet from the fear of changing one's human nature to divine nature, or God, the psyche remains a human psyche as a human mind or soul. If the psyche has to be left as it is, it cannot be changed to actual wisdom, and so the body remains a human body, not God's immortal, formless wisdom body.

TIES TO THE BODY

The Pope also mentions ties existing in the body that join man to external reality, but how can man's body be kept? When man is born, he has the body of an infant, which changes into the body of a young person, an adult, and an old person. So each body must change without staying the same. Also, it is uncertain how long each person will live since it is the result of individual karma. However, whether one lives to an average age or has a long life, the body will continually change as time passes, so how can it be expected to keep a body from changing? Even if many millions of doctors try to keep the body the same, it still changes. Human nature, the psyche, and the body all change even just within one lifetime as an individual progresses from one age to another, so what is it that is supposed to be kept? In the Buddhist tradition, even though one is born with the body of a human being, this tie cannot be kept. How can it be kept, and who can keep it? It may be good for nihilists, who only believe in what is unbelievable because it is changeable, to think they can keep something, but they still cannot keep this tie. Instead of thinking about an impermanent tie and trying to make it permanent, Buddhism teaches detachment from what is impermanent in order to attain the immortal enlightened state through practice and meditation.

The Hinayana doctrine, which is the level of Buddhism the Pope criticizes, teaches that the substantial body causes attachment, and so Hinayana Buddhists believe in breaking ties to the body. However, the Mahayana and Vajrayana doctrines have different points of view about the body and ways of seeing it. In any case, the ordinary body is impermanent. Since human realms have existed, there is no one who can prove that there is one body in this world that has not died. So even if the Pope has the good intention of not breaking the ties of the human body to this world, there is no history of anyone who has not broken ties to the ordinary human body. Of course, this does not include the body of Jesus, whose resurrection and immortality as the son of God occurs at a spiritual level and cannot be discussed in terms of an ordinary flesh body. Buddhism also has many histories of Buddhas with rainbow vajra bodies, which never die.

When the Pope uses the example of the body as evidence for human ties to reality, he acknowledges a connection between reality and the body, but does not connect the body to the mind or see it as created by the mind, as Buddhists do. If the Pope considers the Buddhist view of reality, is he threatened by a loss of reality? According to Buddhism, he is not going to lose anything, because the minds of sentient beings are infinite and can create infinite reality and unreality.

4

INDIFFERENCE, DETACHMENT, AND LOVE

The Pope writes that according to Buddhism,

> to save oneself means, above all, to free oneself from
> evil by becoming indifferent to the world, which is the
> source of evil. This is the culmination of the spiritual
> process. [p. 86]

However, this is a misrepresentation, since the culmination of
Buddhism is liberation from deluded mind that causes karma
and from cyclic existence. Release from the ego is the target.
The Pope seems to be blaming Buddhists for not having compassion and for abandoning the world through detachment.
This is an absurd distortion. It appears that the Pope has decided that this world is real and that Buddhists are giving it
up. However, if the point of view of the reality of the perception of the senses is held in this way, it could even be said that
God and heaven do not exist since many nihilists in this world

do not see them or believe in whatever does not materially appear in front of them.

In his references to Christianity, the Pope feels it is right for Christians to recognize that

"the entire world is subject to precariousness" [p. 56],

"it is subject to corruption and mortality" [p. 56], and

"the world is not the source of man's ultimate happiness. Rather, it can become the source of his ruin" [pp. 55–56].

When Buddhists recognize these same characteristics about the world, the Pope is critical and calls it

"negative soteriology" [p. 85],

"the conviction that the world is bad" [p. 85], and

"awareness of the evil which exists in man's attachment to the world" [p. 87].

Like Christians, Buddhists believe the world is not the source of man's ultimate happiness. But when Hinayana Buddhists believe in this way and practice to attain nirvana, the Pope calls it becoming indifferent to an evil world to attain a state of perfect indifference and says that we do not draw near to God in this way. Does he think we draw near to God by attacking other religions? Even if the Pope does not understand Buddhist detachment, at least he can recognize that it has the compassion not to cause conflict between people and to leave other religions in peace. When the Pope quotes the words of the Bible that God "gave his only son, so that everyone who believes in him might not perish but have eternal life" (p. 184),

I am happy to hear that everyone who believes in Jesus will not perish. Buddhists believe that through their faith in Buddha and through their practice, they can achieve nirvana, which means they will not perish but have eternal life.

Buddhism teaches the importance of tangible and intangible love and compassion both temporarily for the benefit of sentient beings and ultimately for enlightenment. It teaches that the activities of the Bodhisattvas, who have selflessly vowed to attain enlightenment for the benefit of all beings, appear wherever beings exist, which does not mean only in this world where human beings exist. It would seem very limited to Buddhists to have to think that these activities must always appear in a tangible form that is demonstrated in this world. It is impossible to believe in a spiritual point of view if it is thought that everything, including love, must be materially proven in front of people, since it does not always prove anything and may sometimes be something else. When a fisherman wants to catch fish to eat, he uses worms as bait because fish love worms and the fisherman loves fish. Also, a pig who is being fed by a farmer may think the farmer loves him, but the farmer may only love his meat.

If one only believes deeply in material reality, even though it does not have any inherent existence apart from the conceptions of sentient beings, it would mean that even the Holy Spirit could not be considered to exist and function, since it cannot be generally seen within material reality. It must not be decided that spiritual qualities can be only material or only immaterial, since they can be both, depending on intention, temporarily for the happiness of sentient beings and ultimately to liberate them.

The references the Pope makes to Buddhists not caring about and abandoning others are totally inaccurate. It seems that the Pope is suggesting that Buddhists abandon the world out of selfishness. There has never been one word or conception about this in any Buddhist teachings. Within the Hinayana vehicle, when enlightenment is attained and the individual phenomena of the world cease, there is no conception of this world, and there is no perceiver or perception, which means there is no harm or hatred. The detachment of the Hinayana does not mean that the one who is practicing thinks there is a reality world that he leaves when he is practicing, or especially when he attains nirvana. It is not like the divorce of a long-term couple. It means that his own individual dualistic phenomena of samsara have ceased in peace, which does not mean that the general phenomena of the world cease for others, according to the Hinayana.

The word *detachment* is used by both Saint John of the Cross and in the Hinayana vehicle of Buddhism. It is the same word with the same meaning of not clinging to the material world, though perhaps the scope is different for the Hinayana, since their detachment includes all existence. Yet, when the Pope uses the word *detachment* for Buddhists, he gives it the negative meaning of not caring about others and abandoning the world, whereas when Saint John uses the same word, the Pope thinks it means union with a personal God. Does the Pope think that the world is abandoned when there is union with a personal God, or that the material world is carried into a personal union with an immaterial God? If there is union with God without any intention of abandoning the world, then what is wrong with no longer having any phenomena of a world or of a self, which all dissolve into union, as in the nirvana of the Hinayana?

The aspiration of Hinayana practice is never to remain in samsara, the suffering of the circle of existence. The aspiration of Mahayana practice is never to remain in samsara and to attain fully enlightened Buddhahood with immeasurable wisdom mind and wisdom compassion for the benefit of all other beings. So without moving from the state of nondualistic wisdom mind, and at the same time without attachment to the nirvana of personal peace, Buddhas and Bodhisattvas continuously manifest to benefit all beings in many ways, not

only in small, substantial ways, but through the physical ema-
nations of bodies, through the speech of Dharma, and through
the mind of great compassion. It is preposterous to misinter-
pret the word *detachment* in relation to Buddhism to mean
indifference, particularly in light of the Mahayana teachings
in which compassion is the key. That is why Buddha Shakyamuni said,

> *Whoever wants to attain fully enlightened Buddhahood,*
> *Do not learn many things. Only learn one thing.*
> *What is that? It is great compassion.*
> *Whoever has great compassion holds all of the wisdom*
>   *qualities of Buddha in his hand.*

If the Pope is not repelled by the Mahayana teachings, he
can look at them and see that the main teaching, practice, and
path to enlightenment of Mahayana Buddhism is love and
compassion, not only for human beings in this world but for all
sentient beings throughout existence, until all suffering has
ended. This is because until the dualistic mind of sentient beings has ceased, they create countless other realms through
their conceptions, building the habits of unhappiness and happiness, just as even within the conception of a single individual's dream, countless sentient beings can exist. Sentient beings,
which means beings with minds, project the tangible and intangible existence of unending dualistic phenomena. Since sentient beings and their conceptions are infinite, the compassion
of the Buddhas is infinite. That is why Buddha said to liberate
all sentient beings, and not just human beings from this world.

According to the Bodhisattva path of the Mahayana vehicle, until enlightenment, one must take Bodhicitta vows to love
all beings, not only the human beings of this particular world.
When enlightenment is attained, there are no phenomena of
ordinary sentient beings, which come from dualistic habit.
When dualistic habit is purified, without moving from the state

of unshakably abiding in enlightenment, manifestations of wisdom occur unceasingly through unobstructed compassion for all ordinary sentient beings because of the power of previous prayers made over many lives to help beings. When someone plants an apple seed, even if he is no longer there when the seed grows into a tree, the apples still come, again making seeds, which again make apples. Even though the tree has no conception or intention of wanting to give fruit or to fulfill the wishes of beings by the fruit it bears, the result of fruit is there. Likewise, love and compassion arise naturally with spiritual practice and are the inevitable and effortless qualities of enlightenment. The limitless compassion of the activities of the Buddhas is the spontaneous fruit of their previous aspirations over many eons.

The Mahayana teaches one to become sublime in order to be able to care for all beings. This is because through becoming sublime, one has the spiritual power to care for beings for their ultimate benefit, and not only in a material way for their temporary benefit. This caring is not indifference. Developing spiritual power is caring. If the Pope thinks that caring should be demonstrated only in a material way, as nihilist people are thinking it should, then what is the difference between this kind of caring and the caring of politicians who always say they care and talk a lot about what they will do for others? Where is the special spiritual quality and power to care in a profound way? Spiritually empowered caring should be able to occur without having a limitation of one-sidedness or being for only one purpose. It should be always ready to benefit unobstructedly many different beings at a material or nonmaterial level, and not only in a way that is visible or perceptible to others.

The Pope says directly that detachment in Buddhism is indifference to the world. He says that Buddhists

> liberate [them]selves only through detachment from
> the world, which is bad. The fullness of such a detach-

ment is not union with God, but what is called nirvana, a state of perfect indifference with regard to the
world. [p. 86]

Nirvana does not mean indifference, which is a word that
carries the negative connotation of not having any interest in
or concern for others. According to the Hinayana, nirvana is
enlightenment, and enlightenment is Buddhahood. It means
the attainment of sublime peace through the cessation of all
dualistic phenomena by the purification of obscurations. But
the Pope thinks Buddhist detachment from the world is bad,
implying indirectly that it does not include love, and that
Christian detachment is good since it does include love. He
says that Saint John of the Cross

proposes detachment from the world in order to unite
oneself to that which is outside of the world—by this I
do not mean nirvana, but a personal God. Union with
Him comes about not only through purification, but
through love. [p. 87]

This attempt to compare Buddhist detachment unfavor-
ably to Christian love is a surprising parallel, since love is considered to be one of the qualities of enlightened mind according
to the Mahayana. In Vajrayana Buddhism, enlightenment is
often described as the state of the three bodies of the Dharmakaya, the Sambhogakaya,[1] and the Nirmanakaya.[2] The
Nirmanakaya is the embodiment of love, which manifests unobstructedly from the Sambhogakaya and Dharmakaya, ben-
efiting countless beings existing in samsaric phenomena.

In Buddhism, it is said that one must have devotion to and
faith in Buddha, and love and compassion for sentient beings.
If someone truly has love, it automatically creates faith, and if
someone truly has faith, it automatically creates love. It is unnecessary to make faith less important than love, or love less

important than faith. It depends on what is necessary according to time, place, beings, and one's own versatility, circumstances, and positive purpose. In Christianity, God loves the world and the world loves God and prays to God with faith, which means that there is a connection between love and faith. While love and faith can be divided intellectually, they are actually interdependent.

If there is too much stress on substantializing the forms that love is supposed to take, then love can cause hatred, and faith can cause disbelief. Love and faith must have a clear, pure intention. Without a correct point of view and skillful means, if one only talks about love which is supposed to be materially or externally demonstrated, one cannot be sure what love will cause. It is said that patience ages into anger and love ages into hatred.

It is very difficult to recognize actual love. Some people love their God so much that they follow doctrinaire ideas that lead to fighting, killing, and hatred in the name of love. These days, it can be seen that this is happening everywhere. Also, religious doctrines have caused too much wrongful grasping and misinterpretations of love and faith, resulting in genocide. If judged carefully, sometimes what is called the love of God is really the hatred of another religion, when both cause the same essence of killing, grasping, and suffering. Also, some people who do not believe in religion try to destroy others who do believe in religion, killing hundreds of thousands for their love of material power. Many different religions have taught their followers to kill, and they have killed and are killing hundreds of thousands in the name of love and faith, thinking they can be born in heaven. This killing causes suffering, not happiness. So one has to be aware of what love means. It is easy to say the word, but one must be careful that the word matches the meaning.

The Pope writes that Buddhists become indifferent to the

world through detachment, but this is his own projection about the Hinayana vehicle. According to the Pope, if Hinayana practitioners are detached about passions, they are considered not to have love for the world, while if Catholics are detached about passions, they are considered to be moral. I can respect Catholic morality, but to say that the Hinayana has no love, is indifferent, and has a negative approach to the world is disrespectful, misconstruing Buddhism in a negative way while supporting Catholicism in a positive way, even though it is the same issue.

From a spiritual perspective, there are many different kinds of caring. Sometimes what seems to be not caring is caring. Love can assume many aspects. For example, there are hundreds of rules that are connected to the vows of Hinayana monks as taught by Buddha, one of which is to just stand until food is given and not to disturb people. If food is not given, the monks should not wait but, without anger, watch the mind and then go away. This undemanding stance is a form of love. Hinayana practitioners are not asking for anything from the world, and according to the pure Hinayana tradition, they are not supposed to ask for anything in order to accumulate wealth. This giving up of the wish for wealth is generosity, even though it is not called by that name. As Milarepa said, "If there is no coveting, then generosity beyond this does not exist." As long as there is a wish to have something, they give up their wish for it, which is a way of giving to others. Similarly, if someone attacks one's body, not reacting in return is love. If someone says abusive words, not answering back with further abuse is love. It is difficult to say what is not love and what is love. It is subtle.

Apparently, the Pope has not seen Buddhist love with his own eyes or heard about Buddhist love that has been seen through the eyes of his advisors, since he has decided that Buddhists do not love God or the world and humankind, and has blamed Buddhists for this. The Pope's decision that Buddhists are unconcerned with love indicates a complete lack of knowledge or understanding of Buddhism. However, even if the Pope has not seen obvious expressions of reality love in this reality world by Buddhists, that does not mean it does not exist. If one believes only in what is seen, needing substantial proof as though it were evidence for a trial, one should remember how many mistakes are made in courts of law by judges and juries, even though they see and hear reality evidence. If religious people only accept evidence from the world of reality, how can they believe in hell and heaven? If they only accept evidence from the world of reality, they would have to ignore hell and heaven, just as nihilists do. Also, one cannot judge love by what is obviously seen of it. As everyone knows, many husbands and wives may show obvious demonstrations of love for each other, but it does not always mean it is actual love, since they often have hatred for each other and leave each other. What appears to be positive may not be only positive; it sometimes conceals negative energy. If it is thought that only this world is real and that love must be shown in an obvious way that is perceptible through the ordinary senses, then how is love shown by God, without substantial form?

For those of any religion, the meaning of love depends on the capacity of the individual to understand what love actually is and not just what it is announced to be. If one only believes in love that is obviously exhibited, then many other sentiments can be disguised as love, and many kinds of love will go unacknowledged.

If the Pope truly wants to love the world, he has to practice according to the Mahayana and Vajrayana vehicles. Since the Pope does not seem to have heard anything about the Vajrayana vehicle of Buddhism, he does not know that it has countless teachings about the yidam, or personal wisdom God, and countless practices culminating in the attainment of union with the yidam, which is wisdom God undifferentiated from

Buddha. This attainment is imbued with the power of love that extends to countless beings. But if Buddhists try to transform into Buddha with the aspiration to benefit others, which is the ultimate love, the Pope thinks Buddhists are atheists and do not love other beings.

5

ATHEISM

The Pope says,

Buddhism is in large measure an atheistic system. [p. 86]

Atheism means not believing in God, or more generally, not having any spiritual view. The Pope must never have stepped into any Buddhist temples, which are full of images of belief in Buddha. Even though the Pope has not seen the actual Buddha because of his lack of devotion for Buddha, he must know through the evidence of these images that Buddhists believe in Buddha. Even if the Pope has never entered an actual Buddhist temple, he must at least go to a museum with an Asian cultural exhibit that shows Buddhist images such as paintings, statues, and other spiritual art portraying Buddha, which show that others believe in Buddha, and ask a knowledgeable curator, "Why have these images of Buddha happened?" Before the Pope says that Buddhism is atheistic, it would be better for him to consider all the Buddhist objects of veneration that exist in the world, which demonstrate that Buddhism is not atheistic.

Even though the Pope does not accept Buddha, he still has to accept and consider that there is the word *Buddha*. That alone shows that Buddhism has an object of faith and focus, which means it is not an atheistic system. It is strange for the Pope to say,

"Buddha is wrong" [p. 43] or

"Buddha is right" [p. 43],

because by calling Buddha wrong or right, the Pope is accepting that there is a Buddha, which destroys the logic of his statement that Buddhism is an atheistic system. Even though Buddhists follow Buddha, they think that whoever believes in God is religious, and they do not call followers of other religions atheistic.

If the Pope thinks that God does not exist in Buddhism, so that Buddhism is therefore an atheistic system, he should think that actually, in the Hinayana, God is Buddha, even though Buddha is not called God, but Buddha. Also, especially according to the Mahayana and Vajrayana doctrines, the Pope should acknowledge that there are wisdom Gods. The entire Mahayana doctrine is about wisdom Gods. The Vajrayana doctrine has many different teachings at many different levels about *jnana deva,* which is wisdom deity and wisdom God, and how to transform into wisdom deity or wisdom God, including the wisdom deity or wisdom God of the outer tantric teachings, the wisdom deity or wisdom God of the inner tantric teachings, and the wisdom deity or wisdom God of the inconceivable, secret Mantrayana teachings, which is the essence of the fully enlightened phenomena of Buddhas, appearing in myriad aspects as manifestations of the unobstructed, infinite qualities of enlightenment.

Atheists do not believe in karma. If Buddhism were an atheistic system, Buddhists would not believe in karma at all.

Buddhists believe that one can make bad or good karma, that bad karma can be changed to good karma, and that good karma can be changed to no karma when the fully enlightened state of Buddhahood is achieved.

I have heard that in the past, some Christians who were familiar with Buddhism decided that Buddhism was a philosophy and not a religion. These people must have made this decision because they had not had any exposure to Buddhism other than to have learned that philosophical questions are studied by Buddhists. They did not understand the purpose of these studies or know anything about the many other traditions within Buddhism. Perhaps this misinterpretation arose since Buddhists engaged in philosophical debate in monasteries could be observed by visitors, while Buddhists anonymously engaged in prayer and meditation, following other traditions within Buddhism, were less conspicuous. Actually, Buddhism reveals countless methods to attain enlightenment, reflecting innumerable views that will benefit beings, including many different philosophies, but it is not limited to philosophy. Even Buddhist philosophy is unlike ordinary philosophy, since it is entirely spiritual, and its purpose is to guide beings to enlightenment through opening wisdom. However, the Pope is following those Christians who thought of Buddhism as an atheistic philosophy. These days, some Christians are threatened by Buddhism at a spiritual level since it seems more valuable than Christianity, so they try to suppress it by reviving and reinforcing this old, dead, useless, wrong conception about Buddhism, which is like bringing back a zombie.

In Buddhism, the belief in the reality of the world is considered to be related to atheism, since the strong belief in the reality of what can be publicly known through the ordinary senses is the basis of disbelief in what appears as publicly imperceptible to the ordinary senses, but which can be revealed through faith as the senses are transformed through wisdom and can perceive what is beyond ordinary reality. So if the Pope thinks that the world is real and the people of the world are real, it sounds like atheism from the Buddhist point of view. Likewise, if the Pope believes in heaven, he must inadvertently reject the world by believing that heaven is different from this world and aspiring to enter it. If someone falls in love with the reality of the world and humankind, it demonstrates that he does not want to believe in heaven, which is unreal to many reality-thinking nihilists. If the Pope says the world exists tangibly, then does he say that God exists tangibly in the world? If God exists tangibly, the same as other beings, then he can disappear and finish, the same as other beings.

If one unites with God, the conception of the reality of the ordinary world is purified. If the Pope thinks the world exists and cannot be abandoned, then what is the purpose of praying to God without having an aspiration to go beyond the ordinary world? Is heaven different than or the same as this world? How does one unite with God without attaining a state beyond the heavy reality of worldly materialism? In the Hinayana tradition, one must release attachment to this world, realizing egolessness so there is no attachment to a self and therefore no attachment to what is other than self. How can a material man unite with an immaterial God without losing his sense of a material world? Is it like shooting a space shuttle up in the sky for a few weeks, which then has to come back again? If it is like that, it is not an ultimate union.

In conjunction with the Pope's misinterpretation of Buddhist indifference to the world, he says,

Do we draw near to God in this way? This is not mentioned in the enlightenment conveyed by Buddha. [p. 86]

That is because Buddhism follows Buddha. The Pope does not need to be disappointed that Buddhists do not mention getting close to the God of Christianity to attain enlightenment. As

Buddha said, there are many different gods. The acceptance of gods is called eternalism, and disbelief in gods is called nihilism. It is lucky that Buddhists do not mention getting close to God in the sense that the Pope conveys, because the Pope's idea is not actually God according to an eternalist point of view, and not actually nothingness according to a nihilist point of view. It is only a source of confusion. Confusion seems evil because it does not liberate. Sometimes one foot steps on the side of the nihilist point of view, and sometimes one foot steps on the eternalist side. It is hard to move continuously on two sides at once like this, and it is hard to understand how this could lead to unification with God.

6

CREATION

The Pope compares Jesus to Muhammad, Socrates, and Buddha, and says about Jesus,

> Less still is he similar to Buddha with his denial of all that is created. [p. 43]

The Pope denigrates Buddha more than Muhammad and Socrates in order to dignify Jesus. However, the nature and qualities of sublime beings cannot be put on a scale to determine the weight of their worth, as though they had some ordinary value. Nothing can be decided from material conceptions about sublime beings. It is unnecessary to put sublime beings or religions in a contest with each other. Likewise, without studying the teachings of the Buddha, the Pope has judged the religions of the world, which he seems to rank according to their similarity to Christianity. The Pope is like the chairman in charge at the Olympics, giving a gold medal to Christians, a silver medal to Judaism, and a bronze medal to Islam. Buddhism is disqualified, but since all beings have Buddha nature and the potential to attain enlightenment, even though some beings seem less capable due to previous nihilist habit, it is certain that this great potential can someday emerge and develop naturally with good circumstances and that Buddha can become the crown on top of each being's head.

The Pope says,

> Buddha is right when he does not see the possibility of human salvation in creation, but he is wrong when for that reason he denies that creation has any value. [p. 43]

The Buddha does not deny creation. It is only the theory for the basis of creation that is different in Christianity and Buddhism. Christians believe that creation comes from God, "by Whom all things were made" (p. 46), as the Pope quotes from the Nicene Creed. Buddha teaches that creation comes from the minds of beings. The Pope is not right when he says that Buddha denies that creation has any value, since Buddhism always teaches the value of precious human life, which the Pope considers an aspect of creation. Buddhists pray to be reborn in a human body because humans have the special endowment of eight leisures[1] and ten opportunities[2] to attain the state of full enlightenment. In teachings for sentient beings, Buddha shows what is wrong and what is right about their intentions and activities. Buddhism shows how to purify the source of unhappiness, how to cause happiness temporarily in this life, and how to ultimately attain fully enlightened Buddhahood, which means salvation, not only for humankind but for all sentient beings. There is no greater salvation than this.

The Pope says,

> The Creator, from the beginning, saw a multitude of good in creation. [p. 44]

According to Buddhism, through interdependent relative truth, all bad or good circumstances or phenomena are created

64

by mind. Bad phenomena are created by negative conception, and good phenomena are created by positive conception. But the Pope describes Christians as believing in the goodness of creation and Buddhists as seeing only suffering, with the implication that they are not seeing or pursuing goodness. The Pope writes,

> Creation was given and entrusted to humankind as a duty, representing not a source of suffering but the foundation of a creative existence in the world. A person who believes in the essential goodness of all creation is capable of discovering all the secrets of creation, in order to perfect continually the work assigned to him by God. It must be clear for those who accept Revelation, and in particular the Gospel, that it is better to exist than not to exist. And because of this, in the realm of the Gospel, there is no space for any nirvana, apathy, or resignation. Instead, there is a great challenge to perfect creation—be it oneself, be it the world. [pp. 20–21]

The Pope expands the Christian belief in the goodness of creation with the idea that Christians can work to perfect the creations of man and the world in which he lives. By saying that this leaves no space for nirvana, apathy, or resignation, the Pope tries to equate enlightenment with the negative attributes of apathy and resignation. The grouping of these three words together is very strange. The Pope tries to contrast a picture of inspired, productive, creative Christians who work to make the world a better place with a picture of inactive, uncaring Buddhists who have given up on the world and just endure its suffering or try to escape from it.

I respect that the Pope says good comes from God, and I totally believe in that way. However, it is a misconception that Buddhists think that the world is bad and do not want to do anything about it. This misconception implies that God brings what is bad. According to the Pope's own logic, since God created the world, which is seen as bad, and those who see it as bad, instead of blaming Buddhists for this idea, he would have to blame God.

The Pope also thinks that Buddhists are not perfecting themselves and the world. Buddhists believe that good comes from the blessings of Buddha. Because they believe in karma, which is that bad and good are created by the mind, until attaining full enlightenment, Buddhists continuously believe in creating positive conception and virtue in order to accumulate merit, which means to create goodness. Buddhists believe that actual Buddha is always unchangeably, stainlessly pure, and the origin of all pure phenomena.

Even according to relative truth, it is good to see God or Buddha as totally pure. Since Buddhists believe in karma, they acknowledge that their circumstances come from their previous actions and try to change them with merit and accumulation, never blaming sublime beings for being vengeful or punitive. Good continuously increases because the image of the Buddhist aim is very expansive. Confession is an indication of a belief in goodness. It comes from blaming oneself and is done by ordinary beings to sublime beings. When Christians confess, it is a sign that they think God is pure, and that is why they confess their mistakes to him. Likewise, Buddhists confess if they have done something wrong in order to purify it. But if Christians believe that God brings good and that God also punishes them, it means that God is always there ready to react. If God is always reacting, how can one unite with him? If one tries to confess, purify sin, create merit, worship, and have more and more faith, with the original belief that God is always pure, then even though one is not already pure, one can purify all obscurations in order to be liberated to the stainless, inconceivable state of God.

According to Buddhist tradition, because of the point of

view that Buddha is pure, there is nothing that can cause conflict between Buddha and beings. According to relative truth, worshippers may do something wrong, but Buddha can bless them. Flawless Buddha is always there. Even according to relative truth, the object of veneration is always pure, so it is logically easier to create merit with Buddha's blessing. Likewise, if God is believed to be the origin of pure phenomena, countless positive, pure phenomena will be created according to relative truth.

The Pope's description of apathy, resignation, and a denial of creation and goodness in man and the world does not apply to any level of Buddhism. In the Hinayana vehicle, nirvana can be attained with faith, merit, and keen faculties, and its followers practice to purify ego and attachment without denying the world or thinking it is evil. In the Mahayana vehicle, the inherent nature of Buddha is in the mind of all beings, and its followers practice so that this nature can blossom. In the Vajrayana vehicle, the pure nature of appearance is the all-pervading union of Buddha, and its followers practice to recognize this.

Buddhists believe that creation is mind, and the creator is mind. That does not mean that Buddha is ignored. Without mind, where is the knower or the creator or Buddha? How can Buddha be known? If one believes that one's own mind is the creator, one believes that one can create negative conception and its energy, and positive conception and its energy. This is evident and self-proven. It is more powerful to know this, because one is then going to choose positive conception and phenomena and will therefore automatically know these positive phenomena. Even though positive phenomena seem to appear objectively, by realizing these positive phenomena are Buddha, one can worship and pray until even all prayers, the one who prays, and the object to whom one prays become the same. This point of view causes self-encouragement because Buddha is never imagined to be distant, because the object of pure phenomena, which is Buddha, and the subject who knows Buddha become closer and closer until there is no subject of a knower or object to be known, but only inseparable union.

In Buddhism, even though mind is intangible, it continuously exists intangibly as the source of phenomena. Therefore, the nature of mind itself cannot cease. It is impossible for whatever cannot cease not to do anything. Although the Pope believes Buddhists are not doing anything positive, since the nature of mind is unobstructed, even beings who are atheists or nihilists and do not accept spirituality with belief and faith cannot stop their minds, as everyone knows. That is why they are busy. Only the habit of mind is different, whether it is negative or positive. Also, it does not mean that whoever has the aspect of nihilist habit will never believe in anything, since it is only a temporary habit that can change, so there is not a true, actual atheist or nihilist that exists somewhere in reality. There are so many negative and positive words that can be used in order to point to material or spiritual aspects of the mind's unobstructed phenomena, such as sin, virtue, evil, or God, but whatever phenomena are made, the nature of mind is continually and naturally to create.

Of course, the Pope can choose to believe in God as the creator or whatever he wishes, but it is unnecessary for him to be against Buddhists for their beliefs. Since whatever religion is followed is a personal choice made through a previous connection to that religion, it is best to let others go their own way without maligning them so they can naturally reach a higher level of realization.

If there is a negative intention or aim, the result will be negative; this is inverted relative truth. If there is a positive intention or aim, the result will be positive; this is actual relative truth. If there is an intention or aim to reach the goalless goal of full enlightenment by meditating in order not to cling to any positive phenomena so as not to cause attachment again, and accumulating merit in order not to fall into a nihilist point of view, the union of the most sublime, indivisible state of Buddha can be accomplished. Since the intention and aim of Buddhism is temporarily positive and ultimately sublime, the Pope's pessimistic evaluation does not make sense. It is like the ancient story about monkeys in the jungle who mocked humans, thinking they must be some kind of inferior being because they were missing tails.

The Pope's way of describing Buddhism is different from the Second Vatican Council's statements about Buddhism. Perhaps this is because, in the words of the Pope, the Council

> was meant to be open to non-Christian religions, and to reach the whole modern world. [p. 162]

The Pope quotes the Council's document, *Nostra Aetate*, in which it says in relation to other religions,

> The Catholic Church rejects nothing that is true and holy in these religions. [p. 80]

But there is nothing more rejecting than referring to Buddhism as having a "negative soteriology" (p. 85), as the Pope says. Nothing more negative could be said. The Council is quoted as saying, regarding other religions, that

> the Church has a high regard for their conduct and way of life, for those precepts and doctrines which, although differing in many points from that which the Church believes and propounds, often reflect a ray of that truth which enlightens all men. [p. 80]

> The various schools of Buddhism recognize the radical inadequacy of this malleable world and teach a way by which men, with devout and trusting hearts, can become

capable either of reaching a state of perfect liberation,
or of attaining, by their own efforts or through higher
help, supreme illumination. [p. 80]

The Council also mentions a "common soteriological root
present in all religions" (p. 81).

The statements of this Council were much more positive
about Buddhism than the position of the Pope. The Pope should
not have included these ideas from the Council in his book,
because they contradict what he himself says about Buddhism,
since the Pope thinks Buddhist enlightenment is purely negative. Which one is to be believed? One of these sides has to be
deleted for consistency. However, the Pope's negative opinions
are based on a lack of knowledge about Buddhism, which pre-
cludes being able to make any judgments about it, as demonstrated by the Pope's own words. I request that he consider the
words of the Council. Also, as an ancient saying goes, one who
criticizes other doctrines without the support of sublime speech
and one's own incisive logic is like a potter who walks to the
market through a stone-throwing war while carrying his clay
pots on his back.

7

UNION

Even though all of the Pope's references to Buddhism relate to the Hinayana vehicle, which is only a part of Buddhism, the Pope shows that he is unfamiliar with even just the Hinayana in his comments about God and union with God. Even if the word *God* is not used in the Hinayana, whatever liberates into peacefulness is God. For union to occur, it is unnecessary to think that something has to be unified like two people who become husband and wife.

The Pope compares Buddhist detachment from the world to Christian union with God. It is unusual to compare the detachment of one doctrine with the union of another doctrine. However, concerning detachment, if the Pope is attached to the world, what is there to worship? According to Buddhism, if one unites with Buddha, samsara does not exist. If one unites with God, and God is sublime, then one unites with a sublime being, and that means not an ordinary being. If the Pope still wants to be in the material world, it looks like it will be impossible to unite with a sublime God due to grasping ordinary dualistic habit. The Pope refers to his own personal God like a sentient being, with so much attachment to the world. But one cannot be near God no matter how much one prays if one keeps the misconception of the division of distance between the worldly and the sublime.

Union is oneness. Oneness is the origin of all Buddhas. To give a simple example, just as an animal born from the beginning with two horns cannot be made into a unicorn, a dualistic point of view which separates phenomena and results in delusion cannot be made into the union of wisdom. But just as a unicorn is born from the beginning with a single horn, the conception of oneness, which is the belief in the seed of Buddha nature, can blossom into the ultimate union of the result, which is Buddhahood. Union will come because the seed is oneness.

My understanding of the meaning of the words of Saint John of the Cross, which the Pope has included in his chapter on Buddhism, is that if one is not detached from the world, one is not going to unite with God. The Pope quotes Saint John's beautiful poetry, but strangely, if one follows the Pope's words, one would have to conclude that nothing can happen in that way. According to the Pope, if one joins with an invisible God in union, one will lose the ordinary world, and

> it is in the world that man meets God. Therefore he does not need to attain such an absolute detachment [p. 89],

as the Pope says Buddhists do. So according to the Pope, man is supposed to perfect himself and the world, which is the work God gave him to do, without too much detachment, which would be, as the Pope says, against the development of man and the world (p. 88).

However, Saint John says,

> To arrive at what you do not enjoy, you must go where you do not enjoy. [p. 86]

To me, this means that in order to reach that which is not en-
joyed by ordinary mind, one should go to the sublime state not
known by ordinary beings, which is the inconceivable state of
sublime beings. To me, he is showing where to go and asking
one to go there.

Saint John says,

> To reach what you do not know, you must go where
> you do not know. [p. 86]

I would think that to reach what is not known belongs to ordinary beings who do not know what this is, which is the inconceivable state of God. By saying to go where you do not know,
Saint John is telling followers to go to this inconceivable place.
To me, he is showing where to go and asking one to go there.

Saint John says,

> To come into possession of what you do not have, you
> must go where now you have nothing. [p. 86]

He is directing and requesting that one must go to the inconceivable state of which one does not yet have awareness. To me,
he is showing where to go and asking one to go there.

As previously discussed, the Pope says that Buddhist liberation "necessitates a break with the ties that join us to external
reality" (p. 85). However, if Saint John "proposes detachment
from the world in order to unite oneself to that which is outside
of the world" (p. 87), it is suddenly all right to be detached
from the world, though it seems to be right only for Christians
and not for Buddhists, and it suddenly becomes positive to the
Pope, if it is for Christians, because as the Pope says, it is not
nirvana but a personal God.

> Union with Him comes about not only through purifi-
> cation, but through love. [p. 87]

Union with Buddha also comes through purification and love. The word *Buddha* means not only the purification of all obscurations but also the attainment of all enlightenment qualities, which includes the immeasurable love of great compassion for all beings. Buddha is the embodiment of love.

It is unsuitable to refute the detachment of the Hinayana by comparing it with Christian love and union with God. Perhaps this has been done because in the Christian view that the Pope extols, it seems that love is not having to give up anything, but being attached, like something between a girlfriend and a boyfriend, creating more attachment and causing more suffering. In Buddhism, love is not seen as a honeymoon. When beings become sublime, they are detached through their weariness of samsara. This detachment occurs because the mind becomes sublime. When the mind is sublime, it has greater power to actually help sentient beings with the energy of divine love.

According to the Vajrayana, union is the main practice to attain enlightenment. The ultimate union is becoming the same as Buddha. In Buddhism, union is not substantial, but indivisible as in the union of impalpable appearances and the wisdom of great emptiness. Enlightenment is the state of indivisible union. Buddhists believe that not only man but all sentient beings have the potential to unite with Buddha. The aim of Mahayana Buddhism is to guide all beings throughout all existence to that union with great compassion.

Comparing Buddhist detachment to the detachment of Saint John of the Cross, the Pope says that Saint John

does not conceive of that detachment as an end in itself [p. 86],

showing yet another misconception about Buddhism, since detachment has never been considered an end in itself in Buddhism.

The Pope quotes the Council's *Gaudium et Spes*, which states that the world is

> destined, according to the divine plan, to be transformed and to reach its fulfillment. [p. 89]

He also writes,

> The truth about God the Creator of the world and Christ the Redeemer is a powerful force which inspires a positive attitude toward creation and provides a constant impetus to strive for its transformation and perfection. [p. 88]

If the world is supposed to be transformed and we are supposed to make an effort for it to become perfect, it sounds hopeful that man may be allowed to transcend ordinary reality. But since the Pope writes that man meets God in the world, it sounds as though he is supposed to stay in the world after all; and since the Pope writes that man does not need such an absolute detachment, detachment is still criticized (p. 89). However, if Saint John is detached from the external world, then the Hinayana is at least Saint John's close friend. His poetry sounds like it is Buddhist. Saint John wants to unite with a personal God; Hinayana practitioners want to attain a personal nirvana. The goal is the same; only the names of God and Buddha are different.

Most of the Pope's criticisms of Buddhism can be synthesized in the inference that Buddhism has a negative attitude and Christianity has a positive attitude. But he uses a very flexible form of argument to try to prove this, emphasizing again and again his support of the Christian view with proof that would also apply to Buddhism, as well as impugning the Buddhist view with contentions that either would apply to Christianity or do not apply at all to Buddhism. He also twists the same topic into something negative if it is in relation to Buddhism, and into something positive if it is in relation to Christianity. He seems to be preoccupied, since he does not appear to notice that this is illogical. I can only think that this is characteristic of nondual wisdom mind, beyond relying on any theory or logic, so I feel very happy and optimistic about the Pope.

If one wants to join with God through prayer and meditation, it means one will become naturally detached from this external world. This detachment is a sign of a much more profound union than could be accomplished if one were to remain attached to the world. Even though it seems to others that millions of beings are left in the general external world, all phenomena of an external or internal world vanish in the state of union. Actually, the world can vanish not only from practice, when ordinary phenomena relinquish their hold on the mind due to the blossoming of wisdom, but also from the death and destruction of seriously sectarian interests, which cause politically motivated religious conflict and war. If the Pope compares the pain, injury, suffering, and death caused by religious wars to the cessation of suffering that is the result of Hinayana practitioners reducing their attachment to ordinary reality, what does he consider to be right?

The Pope is always considering this world, saying that one should not be detached from this world and that good in the world comes from God. If he thinks good that comes from God must come at a material level, when considering the thousands of deaths among the followers of Catholicism in wars connected with the Church, it seems that not only material good comes. It is even more illogical if this is explained as the punishment of God, since these followers are fighting, killing, and having wars through their faith in God. It is impossible to think that God would betray His followers, who pray to a living God but are then punished by Him, isn't it? I believe that good comes from God, which means that through the karma of sentient beings, good comes to them from their faith, and they have the capacity to accept it. Likewise, good comes from Buddha. It depends on the actions of sentient beings, their karmic fate, and on what they misunderstand or understand. Buddha Shakyamuni said to his followers that they must have faith in Buddha. If sentient beings listen to the speech of Buddha, it naturally creates positive energy through believing in its goodness so that good comes through the power of positive interdependent circumstances. But even though it was not created by Buddha or by God, what is bad can come through sentient beings not having faith. Also, whether or not the goodness of God comes depends on the followers of God and whether or not they have misinterpretations. It is necessary to have the blessing of God, and then good can come.

The Pope's implication is that good comes from God, but never from Buddha. However, the Pope can read and become familiar with Buddha's speech and see how it is taught that merit, which is goodness, can be accumulated not only for this short life but until attaining the state of full enlightenment.

Union with Buddha does not mean anything similar to a union in which God must be God, someone must pray to Him, and then they must unite as in an embrace. Union is more than drawing near or getting close. Drawing near can be said to be on the path to enlightenment, and is not only staying near and never uniting, but getting closer and closer, drawing nearer and nearer. When enlightenment is attained, then there is no more drawing near. Nearness means that duality still exists, since there are still two things in relation to each other. It is actual, total union, not just someone sitting next to God. Dualistic habit is completely purified in the purely mystical state of totally becoming inconceivable Buddha. From the Mahayana perspective, through the accumulation of merit, one first tries to purify negative and dualistic phenomena and to expand nondualistic wisdom phenomena. That means drawing nearer and nearer to Buddha until purely abiding with Buddha in nondualistic wisdom mind with nondualistic wisdom phenomena, only known by Buddha himself. There are no other knowers, not in union or in union. According to the Pope, it seems as if in a union between God and man, the individual definition of each must be preserved, rather than surpassed. As the Pope says,

> In the sphere of the everyday, man's entire life is one of "co-existence"—"thou" and "I"—and also in the sphere of the absolute and definitive: "I" and "THOU." [p. 36]

For Buddhists, there is no division in the sphere of the absolute. From the Buddhist point of view, whatever the essence of God is called, it is supposed to be inexpressible, inconceivable, nonsubstantial wisdom. Until attaining that state of union, one prays, worships, does good deeds, and meditates. But is God always supposed to be left separately and a person left separately praying? That is not negative, but if one changes and gets closer to God, then the one who is praying can become the same as God. That is infallible union. That means, according to Buddhist tradition, there is no "I" and there is no "Thou." When "I" is not left subjectively, "Thou" is not left objectively. If one only says Buddhism does not have a God because, according to my understanding of the Pope's words, God is always supposed to be God and the one who prays is always supposed to be praying, how can they unite? They may get near, but they cannot unite. One cannot be near God, no matter how much one prays, if one keeps this division. They will remain separate like two mountains. It is said,

> *There a mountain, here a mountain;*
> *They are seen by each other, but they never join.*

The Pope quotes the Council as saying,

> When the Lord Jesus prays to the Father so that "they may be one" (Jn 17:22), He places before us new hori-

zons impervious to human reason and implies a similarity between the union of divine persons and the union
of the children of God in truth and charity. [p. 201]

I thought that since Jesus is the son of God, Jesus and God are
already indivisible. Although Jesus appears within the aspect
of form in order to help other beings who exist within form,
the spirit is indivisible. I really do not understand how the Pope
sees Jesus praying. Does he think that Jesus is still praying to
be in union with God, or still waiting? Does the Pope not think
that this may be skillful means or a technique, since Jesus was
born in human form in order to help others, to show others
what they can do in order to become one with God? Buddhists
believe that whatever is said to be a human quality in a sublime
being is actually a wisdom quality manifesting in an aspect to
help humankind. Jesus is not an ordinary human, because he is
the son of God, or a manifestation of God, and God is the state
of inconceivable wisdom, beyond what is sensory or cognitive.

According to the point of view of being on the path to enlightenment, until becoming actual Buddhas, Buddhists pray
and practice to unite with Buddha. According to the point of
view of having accomplished the result of enlightenment,
which is the fruit of the mystical union attained through prayer
and meditation, one becomes Buddha.

8

MYSTICISM

In Buddhism, pure mysticism comes at the level of being on the path to enlightenment, when the mind becomes more and more pure, until it becomes totally pure so there is not even one conception of dualistic habit left, which is the total attainment of full enlightenment. But the Pope writes that in a comparison of Christian mysticism and Buddhism, there is a

> fundamental difference. Christian mysticism . . . is not born of a purely negative "enlightenment." [p. 87]

According to Buddhist tradition, mind is the source of all that is negative and positive, and whichever appears is the choice of beings. The Hinayana Buddhist teachings introduce the importance of purifying negative intention through practice and developing positive intention. There are many wonderful biographies that tell about the spiritual accomplishments, prescient awareness, and miraculous activities of Hinayana mystics, especially when they attained the state of Arhat, the Hinayana state of enlightenment. Before these mystics went to beg for food or to teach, they first examined what would happen. If they saw that negative circumstances would be caused by the negative phenomena of others, such as seeing that others would be harmed by their own negative conception, they would not go. If something positive would be caused through the positive phenomena of others, then they would go.

Since Christian mysticism does not come from a purely negative enlightenment, where does the Pope's negativity about Buddhism come from? His strong condemnation of Buddhism is a sign of not having understood mysticism. If the Pope is intentionally trying to turn people against Buddhism, though it does not mean that all Christians would do this, is it negative or positive? Is it astonishing that the Pope would portray Buddhism so negatively, whether for the purpose of converting people to Catholicism or preventing them from becoming Buddhist? The Pope can have the authority over Catholics to interpret his own doctrine of Christianity, but not Buddhism. If he creates issues about other doctrines, it can cause refutability.

As mentioned before, it is taught in the Mahayana that each being has Buddha nature and the potential to become enlightened whenever the right circumstances blossom through faith and devotion. According to the Vajrayana, through visualization of Buddhas or wisdom deities, Vajrayana practitioners can change previous karmic energy to spiritual wisdom phenomena. These are all completely positive points of view. So actually, Buddhist mysticism comes from an inherent, purely positive enlightenment. It can be said it is purely negative to discourage others from being Buddhist and sabotage their potential to attain enlightenment.

The Pope says,

Carmelite mysticism begins where Buddhism ends. [p. 87]

I believe that Christian mysticism exists because anything can appear according to the different phenomena of sentient beings, including unlimited appearances of spirituality, and anything can be said about them, wrong or right. But does the Pope know where Buddhism ends? Even if one only reads the texts of Buddha Shakyamuni, one can know that until all of cyclic existence becomes empty, the manifestations of the Buddhas are not going to end. Buddha Shakyamuni, the fourth Buddha, is one manifestation from at least one thousand fully enlightened Buddhas who have been named. According to the Mahayana, there are also actually countless Buddhas beyond those who have been named. However many sentient beings exist, that many teachings of Buddhism will come. Until sentient beings end, Buddhism will not end. That is the prayer of the Bodhisattvas and the activity of the Buddhas. Even in this world, although Buddha Shakyamuni came and turned the wheel of Dharma, beings may only see that Buddhas come at particular places and times but not perceive them at other places and times, due to their karma and lack of faith, yet Buddhas are always everywhere. According to the Mahayana texts, each sentient being has Buddha nature. Buddha nature may be dormant, but it never ceases until enlightenment is attained and can be rekindled at any time with good circumstances, such as believing in and having faith in Buddha and the reflections of Buddha nature, hearing the speech of Buddha, seeing Buddha, and meeting sublime teachers and their teachings. Then the Buddha phenomena within one's mind will open.

Buddhist mysticism has to do with intangible, hidden spiritual qualities and exists continuously until all sentient beings are enlightened. It is not hidden with the intention of keeping it secret, but as a protection from misinterpretation and misunderstanding, according to the level of the path to enlightenment. Buddhism teaches that the arcane nature of actual mysticism can pervade within both the material and immaterial, and not only one-sidedly within the material. If the Pope believes in mysticism, he should believe less in the reality of the external world. These two are totally different. Even the Pope's praise of Christian mysticism, thinking it is greater than Buddhist mysticism, is made less viable by seeing the world in such a limited way rather than accepting, as Buddhism does, the immeasurable possibilities of existence and the immeasurable possibilities of the aspects of mysticism that can appear.

If the Pope were to read Buddhist texts, he would discover how the activities of Buddha are boundless and continuous, occurring with limitless skillful means. I thought that this was the most supreme mysticism. The Carmelites should not wait for the end of Buddhist teachings, because it is going to delay their own teaching. Is it possible for the Pope not to expect an end of Buddhism? I do not understand why the Pope said his astounding words about Buddhism being opposed to Christianity (p. 85), and why he did not just leave it that Buddhism is different from Christianity, corresponding to different individual phenomena. Instead of trying to erase Buddhism and having disagreements in many ways with other religions even if they share one God, he should consider that those who are in other religions at least believe in something.

The Pope says, referring to the "culmination of the spiritual process" (p. 86) in Buddhism, which is misrepresented as detachment and indifference, that

> at various times, attempts to link this method with the
> Christian mystics have been made. [p. 86]

However, the Pope proposes that Christian detachment is different from Buddhist detachment. Also, the Pope brings in the words of Saint John of the Cross, saying that they have been "interpreted as a confirmation of Eastern ascetic methods" (p. 86), and tries to negate this by making the intention of Christian detachment seem better than the intention of Buddhist detachment by connecting it to union, love, and God, while not acknowledging the Buddhist emphasis and teachings on union, love, and Buddha, as previously explained.

It does not make sense to compare Buddhist detachment and asceticism with Christian mysticism, as the Pope has done. Of course, there is no objection to practicing detachment, but detachment cannot be used as a description of Buddhist mysticism that is to be compared with Christian mysticism. Also, when the Pope mentions in his chapter on Buddhism that in Eastern Asia, comparisons have been made (although he does not specifically say by Buddhists) between Eastern ascetic methods and the writings of Saint John of the Cross, I do not understand the connection. It seems that the Pope is implying that ascetic methods are an important part of Buddhism. However, asceticism is not the high point of mysticism in Buddhism at all. Although the Hinayana has ascetic practices, which they only consider an outer method and not an ultimate target, the hardship of asceticism is not even part of the Mahayana or Vajrayana teachings or methods.

However, if the Pope wants to consider only the methods of asceticism in Hinayana Buddhism, even they could be connected with mysticism and disprove the Pope's inferences. The Hinayana has methods with many ascetic styles that are impossible for common people to do, even regarding qualities of behavior, including two hundred and fifty root vows for monks to discipline their bodies' behavior, their speech, and their minds, such as not losing mindfulness, as well as how to deal with any worldly circumstance, taming and refining their senses in limitless ways. Confidence in Hinayana mysticism, which is achieving the state of miraculous activity through shamatha[1] and vipasana[2] meditation, including the four miracles, is extremely difficult to accomplish unless one is an exceptional Hinayana follower of the Buddhas. It cannot be understood if one is totally connected with conspicuous thinking and obvious substantialization. When these Hinayana practitioners attain confidence, the result of their mystical accomplishments may be to inconspicuously abide in a sublime state or conspicuously reveal qualities that are absent from the phenomena of ordinary people, such as flying in the sky, until attaining the enlightened Arhat state, or nirvana. In the time of Buddha Shakyamuni, many monks flew in the sky and also knew the faculties of others due to the purification of their heavy karmic energy, including knowing what to teach others according to their individual capacities.

I do not know what the Pope recognizes as mysticism, but if it is defined in a simple way, mysticism is spiritual phenomena beyond ordinary understanding. Of course, Christianity has its own history about God, the Holy Spirit, and Jesus because they are sublime, and also not only about them, but about their teachings and pure followers. But that does not necessarily disprove Buddhist mysticism or mean that since Buddhist mysticism is different from Christian mysticism, it is therefore false. If the Pope could have a little faith in Buddhism, he would know how vast and actually positive Buddhist mysticism is, instead of rejecting it or even refusing to look at or listen to its history.

If the Pope thinks that Christian mysticism is different from Buddhism, how does he know this? The Pope does not know about Buddhist mysticism at all, so it is very early for him to say what it is. Does the Pope think the activity of the Holy Spirit belongs to mysticism or materialism? If it belongs to material behavior, then it is not mysticism. If it is not predictable or recognizable by ordinary beings and functions for the benefit of humankind, then it belongs to mysticism. We are not supposed to say these different kinds of activity are the same; they are not the same. If the Pope thinks the activity of the Holy Spirit is not easily understood, how does he decide at what point Buddhist mysticism is understood enough to be able to devalue it? If the Pope believes in spiritual mysticism, whether it is Catholic or Christian or whatever it may be, even if the Pope does not know the explanations and history of Buddhist mysticism and does not have faith in it, he is logically supposed to have the idea that its meaning may not be understood. He is supposed to accept that mysticism can exist that is beyond understanding, if he is truly connected to spiritual, intangible, mystical ideas. If one believes in mysticism and has a spiritual point of view, one must accept infinite possibilities of how mystical appearances can occur, just as the Pope accepts that the activity of the Holy Spirit can manifest in other religions, and Buddhists believe wisdom activity can manifest in whatever way will connect to beings to open their own wisdom qualities. One should not try to prevent mystical appearances that are not yet understood or do not conform to what one already knows. The Pope's praise of Christian mysticism and his attempt to disprove Buddhist mysticism shows a general refusal to accept spiritual manifestations of mysticism unless they specifically fit into a Christian mold, which is thought somehow to be in a different category. This is like some vegetarians who say they do not eat meat but do eat fish.

The Pope mentions that the Vatican Council recommended dialogue with Moslems, and the Church has tried to be open to it, but he hints that Moslems did not open in response (pp. 93–94). The Pope also mentions that there have been attempts to link Christian mysticism with Buddhism (p. 86), but according to the Pope, there is no link. My guess is that these problems are only coming from too much sectarianism, heightening one's own point of view above the view of others and creating paranoia between those who have different views. The main key is that these problems are not from God or Buddha, but from followers of God or Buddha building an excessively fanatical point of view through a lack of wisdom mind and too much self-righteous ego; or, it has to do with religious politics and not with spirituality or wisdom, so it causes disagreement and distance because of paranoia.

Actually, this particular idea of linking is not connected with wisdom and seems to be connected with manipulation, to promote Catholicism. However, if some people have tried to link Christian mysticism with Buddhism through material

ideas but could not make a link, it was because they were trying to link obvious intellectual conceptions to inconceivable
Buddhist mysticism, and what is obvious cannot be linked
with what is inconceivable. Of course, there are material ideas
and also immeasurable, inconceivable ideas of spiritual teachings both in Buddhism and in Christianity, so there could be
many possible ways of linking them, if the Pope and other religious leaders truly had a positive dedication toward beings to
do this. Yet if the Pope is unable to connect ideas due to holding a point of view of not wanting to link with others, how can
he expect to connect with an immaterial, formless God even
within his own point of view?

Perhaps the Pope should clearly explain what mysticism is,
which is intangible and therefore enigmatic from the perspective of ordinary human understanding, instead of just saying
these confusing words. The Pope proves with his own words
that Buddhism is hidden from himself and his followers by the
discussion of his inability to see any link between Christian
mysticism and Buddhism. The mysticism of Buddhism is so
profound that it cannot be linked to what is obvious and contained within ordinary conception. According to the Pope's
logic, the mysticism of Christianity is obvious and not beyond
ordinary thought because it is contained within conceptions of
attributes that can be explained and compared in order to negate the attributes of other kinds of mysticism.

Buddhist mysticism exists in both the causal and resultant
vehicles. In the mysticism of the causal Mahayana vehicle, the
basis of Buddha nature intrinsically abides within ordinary
mind. It is only hidden because it is not recognized, but this
basis is, from the beginning, mystical. With the aim to attain
enlightenment, there are so many prayers that can be said with
deep devotion in order to benefit countless beings, within
groups or individually, and many methods of the path of enlightenment that can be applied that are beyond ordinary
thought and are not easily understood by ordinary beings. So

according to the level of the path of enlightenment, Buddhist mysticism is extremely vast. When intrinsic Buddha nature opens through prayers, worship, blessings, and meditation, dualistic habit is reduced and nondualistic wisdom phenomena expands. But this is for fortunate beings. Unfortunate beings who cannot see it or conceive of it cannot revalue Buddha nature in this way.

According to the point of view of the basis, one recognizes intrinsic Buddha nature and its phenomena. Then one practices according to the path of enlightenment, and Buddha phenomena become more and more clear. Finally, unobstructed Buddha phenomena appear impalpably, and there is no subjective recognition of Buddha nature because there is no subjective practitioner, since the one who prays and the object of prayer become an indivisible union. At that time, which is timeless, not one conception of mysticism remains, but there is the natural activity of unceasingly pervasive wisdom manifestations, which is the result. These are the basis, path, and result of Buddhist mysticism. More than these, the basis, path, and result become oneness. There is so much that needs to be learned about these, and not only learned, but practiced with many skillful means. But I do not want to cause the Pope to have insomnia. The mystical wisdom power of the Buddhas cannot be found with ordinary calculations. It is impossible because it is unimaginable.

Hinayana mysticism, Mahayana mysticism, and Vajrayana mysticism with inconceivable wisdom deity phenomena cannot be understood unless someone is most fortunate. Even if one tries to materially prove mysticism or make it evident to ordinary discernment, it is not known at all.

The Pope writes that Christian mysticism

has built up and continues to build up Christianity[,] . . . the Church[,] . . . [and] civilization, particularly "Western civilization," which is marked by a positive approach to

the world, and which developed thanks to the achievements of science and technology, two branches of
knowledge rooted both in the ancient Greek philosophical tradition and in Judeo-Christian Revelation.
[p. 88]

It seems a little odd that the value of Christian mysticism is
being substantiated by its influence on scientific and technological achievements, and that this credit is being shared with
the ancient Greeks. Again, the importance of the material
world is stressed, and mysticism is being shown as making its
contribution to civilization, which is human cultural and so-
cial development and not its spiritual development. Again, the
Pope does not want the world to be left or denied but wants it
to be developed. Yet this emphasis reduces the profound nature
of spirituality. Of course, spirituality can enhance any level of
awareness, including appearances within ordinary reality, but
why is that level given so much importance? It is also peculiar
that in other chapters on other subjects within the same book,
the Pope's view of science and technology is presented differently, sounding very much like the Pope's presentation of the
Buddhist view in his chapter on Buddhism:

This world which appears to be a great workshop in
which knowledge is developed by man, which appears
as progress and civilization, as a modern system of
communications, as a structure of democratic free-
doms without any limitations, this world is not capable
of making man happy. [p. 56]

But it seems that the Pope considers the advancement of civilization as making an important contribution to religion when
he quotes the *Nostra Aetate,* the document that defines the
Church in relation to other religions, which says,

Religions that are tied up with cultural progress strive
to solve these issues with more refined concepts and a
more precise language. [p. 79]

The Pope also implicitly discriminates between the East
and the West, alluding to something that is missing from Eastern culture in relation to Western civilization and

the achievements of Western civilization through science and technology. [p. 88]

However, the Pope does not know the dimensions of the culture of the East, which he judges with worldly Western standards. Even in the example of science, whoever studies Buddhist
science properly will find that there is not even one subject
missing in its categorization of all immeasurable knowledge
into five root sciences and five branch sciences. But if the Pope
does not want to look at the extremely extensive Buddhist sciences, as though science does not even exist in the East, since
he considers science important, he should look at what one of
the most famous scientists in the world, Albert Einstein, said
about Buddhism:

The religion of the future will be a cosmic religion. It
should transcend a personal God and avoid dogmas
and theology. Covering both the natural and the spiritual, it should be based on a religious sense arising
from the experience of all things, natural and spiritual,
as a meaningful unity. Buddhism answers this description. . . . If there is any religion that would cope with
modern scientific needs, it would be Buddhism.

If the Pope wants his spiritual leadership to be continuous,
it is unwise to seriously align Catholicism with Western civilization,

science, and technology. Just as many worldly political leaders have tried to create a nonaligned movement in order to make peace in this world, it would also be better for the Pope to be nonaligned instead of trying to connect his religion with the materialism of civilization, science, and technology. Because these are facets of material existence, they will not be continuous but will change.

It is also unwise for the Pope to choose between the East and the West. It is presumptuous to assume that the West is more developed and therefore better, or that its scientific and technological ideas indicate a permanent superiority, since there is nothing about these ideas that can guarantee that they are ultimate or will always be considered the best. Even though circumstances or conditions may temporarily seem better in one place or another, it does not mean they will stay that way forever. In the same way, I cannot say that Eastern religion is always better. Since Buddha nature inherently exists in each being, it is only through a lack of faith, belief, and practice that it remains dormant in Western nihilists, and it is certain that someday, since they have this Buddha nature, it can be revived through good circumstances. It does not matter if someone has blue or brown eyes, or blond or black hair. It is also unwise if Easterners try to align themselves with one another by being racist and saying Westerners are impossible, since it is only momentarily that Westerners have the obstacle of the enormous ego of ordinary human nature and so are not rekindling their Buddha nature.

The Pope's condescension toward Eastern culture and smugness about Western culture is unwise not only because it reveals his lack of interest in Eastern culture, but also because there are many Christians in the East, such as in South Korea, Vietnam, and the Philippines, who will think that the Pope is excluding them because he is racist. This kind of attitude may create doubt for the future, causing Catholics to become Protestants as has been happening in Latin America, resulting in depression for the Pope.

It may sound positive when the Pope writes about the positive attitude of Christianity (p. 88), but his way of using comparisons between his descriptions of Christianity and Buddhism is actually completely negative. It is negative because it is being used to seed negative energy through strongly implying that Buddhism is negative and Christianity is positive. Actually, this point of view is feeding a new cause for two sides to fight in this world. No matter who has a positive attitude and who has a negative attitude, Christians and Buddhists still live together in this world. But the Pope is trying to ensure that this negativity, which is naturally erasable, will become an unerasable fact, even though it is a mistaken conception. Why does the Pope want to build a splendid, perishable sand castle like this that will naturally fall apart? Also, if one considers this conception of negativity as it is presented by the Pope, how can it be made into perfection as God wishes? If Christ is defeating evil according to a divine plan, then why is the Pope planting the idea that Buddhism is negative? Are Buddhists forgotten or left by Christ? That would mean that God does not have an infallible quality that can extend to everyone and would contradict the Council's position in *Nostra Aetate* that

> there is only one community, and it consists of all peoples. [p. 78]

Even though the Pope thinks science and technology are rooted in ancient Greek philosophical traditions and Judeo-Christian revelation, it is unnecessary to think that making a connection between religion and science is spiritually meaningful. Although maybe some scientists believe in religion, including Christianity and creation, many do not. So although the Pope said Christianity was connected to science, using this for the aggrandizement of the West, many scientists are disconnected from spiritual ideas and methods and disbelieve them. It is good for the Pope to visualize that there is a connection, but if reality is considered as the Pope wishes, many scientists do not see an association between science and spirituality. Of course, there are many spiritual scientists, but also many nonspiritual scientists who think they made their achievements themselves from their own effort, not by relying on divine inspiration.

Also, since it is uncertain whether the result of developments that come from science and technology are actually always positive, it is unwise to say that science and technology come from one's religion. As the Pope knows, so many weapons and nuclear bombs that can destroy the world have been invented by scientists, and no one knows what will happen in the world now because of these products of science. By boasting about a connection between religion and science, the Pope seems to have forgotten about nuclear bombs and Hiroshima, as though he is hiding bitter poison under his feet and showing sweet candy in his hand. The personal detachment of a Hinayana practitioner from the world for the purpose of attaining enlightenment himself is much better than the use of science for the purpose of destroying the world. But it sounds as if the Pope likes Western civilization, science, technology, and ancient Greek philosophy better than Eastern religion, and particularly Buddhism. That is not a problem for Buddhists, because it is a different point of view and just a temporary judgment from momentary circumstances. As Buddha Shakyamuni said:

> *Whoever one is considering to be one's mother,*
> *That is another's wife.*
> *What one is considering to be absolute truth,*
> *That is another's relative truth.*

The Pope proposes that one has to have a positive attitude toward the world and to constantly try to make the world better (p. 88). This view is not at all opposed to teachings in Buddhism according to relative truth, even though the Pope tries to present Buddhism differently. But if the Pope thinks that one can actually expect to reach the goal of the transformation and perfection of creation, is that perfection beyond striving? If the aim is only to strive, and striving is considered too important to give up, how can one ever reach perfection?

In every vehicle of Buddhism, there is an emphasis on the goal. Buddhists see this as very positive. Of course, even trying and striving for this goal is positive, and there are countless benefits at a relative level from doing so, but there are also many teachings about actually reaching this goal, which show that it is possible to reach it. This is a totally optimistic, positive view. The goal is enlightenment. The three main doctrines of Buddhism can each be approached from the three levels that were previously described of the basis, the path, and the result, and whatever explanation is given about any topic within any of these doctrines can use the logic of any or all of these three levels. At every level, Buddhism is always rich, always profound, and always clear. Although it is described differently according to the level of the teaching, the result at every level is enlightenment. In the Vajrayana, the result of enlightenment must be developed by seeing that the result is itself the seed. Since the result is already there, one must only have faith and develop it from recognition. Although there is not much discussion of detachment as one might find in the Hinayana, there is a lot about great emptiness, which is the essence of the sky of wisdom. By seeing the pure essence of appearances, there is no need for detachment or abandoning the world. By seeing that everything is empty, one is not going to grasp phenomena, yet phenomena are already there, not needing to be left. Nonsubstantial appearances are occurring, indivisible from great emptiness wisdom. That is why they are naturally peaceful and full of exaltation.

The Pope makes a connection between Christian mysticism and love, describing what can be shown in front of the world to prove the value of the mysticism of Christianity. But if the value of mysticism is confirmed only by what is demonstrated tangibly to the world, it does not mean that it then becomes actual mysticism. Mysticism is hidden and intangible. Although the Pope believes in Christian mysticism, his focus seems to be on this tangible world, and it is impossible to find mysticism only within what is tangible. If one is sealed within the tangible by belief in substantial reality, which is inherently limited, one cannot open to pure mysticism, which is incomprehensible through ordinary conceptual thought because it comes from the all-pervading limitlessness of wisdom. According to the Buddhist point of view, mysticism can exist anywhere, anytime, within substance and nonsubstance, as many positive phenomena. In any religion, mysticism is supposed to be positive, since it only comes from the power of the blessing of wisdom, from God or Buddha.

The Pope seems to be trying to make Buddhism look bad in front of normal people who have the habit of believing in substance and who are inexperienced about the nonsubstantial spirituality of Buddhism, in order to make them doubt Buddhism. Although the Pope cautions others against becoming detached from this world, if one does not become detached from this world, then there is no quality of mysticism. Since mysticism is the personal experience of intangible spiritual qualities, and since this personal recognition is itself intangible, how can one recognize and develop this experience if one has to remain within the tangible world?

The Pope talks about the ways in which Christian and Buddhist mysticism are different. Of course, there are many Buddhist mystics and scholars who know what Buddhist mysticism is and how it could be differentiated from other mystical traditions if it were beneficial to do so. However, the differences which the Pope enumerates are inaccurate and uninformed. Actually, Buddhist mysticism begins where the Pope's obscured reflection of Buddhism ends. Whoever reads about mysticism in the Mahayana teachings and especially the Vajrayana teaching will either panic from misinterpreting them or be filled with positive awe from correctly understanding the enormity of Buddhist mysticism, from which they can benefit directly and indirectly. One must read and study these teachings; it is not enough to just glance at one book or listen to old, inaccurate clichés and hearsay about Buddhism. If one goes too far to criticize another religion without examining it carefully, it can be dangerous, just as if a man blows excessively on a fire and the fire suddenly flames back at him, it can burn his mustache.

9

RELIGIONS

As the Pope mentions in the beginning of his chapter on Buddhism, the attitude of being open-minded appeals to many modern people, who appreciate it when worldly democratic and political ideas about freedom are applied to religion. These days, people mix up their supposedly complementary substantial conceptions, which are not really pure spiritual ideas, by trying to blend different points of view, ways of worship, and ways of practice in a melting pot of religions. But an actual synthesis of different religious traditions can be done only through the naturally complementary energy of spiritual realization and not through this kind of mixing of the contradictions of ordinary ideas. Buddhism is a complete religion, not an addition to another religion, and Christianity is also. It just causes a lot of confusion rather than clarity to try to combine them, just as if Coke and Pepsi are mixed together, there is no taste. However, the Pope is not only cautioning Catholics not to mix religions with each other since it can cause confusion, but is trying to present a negative picture of Buddhism, as though he is afraid it has too much appeal and may draw his own followers away, so that he must give Buddhism particular consideration. The Pope says,

It is necessary to give special attention to Buddhism [p. 84],

which means a special attack. It sounds as though the Pope is afraid that Buddhism will flourish. It is a contradiction to be teaching how to be saved from fear and go to heaven, but then to continue to create more fear.

The Pope does not need to worry that Catholics will be taken over by Buddhists. Buddhism is very precious, and unless one is very lucky, one cannot meet the Buddhist teachings, which liberate oneself and help other beings at the same time. But even though there are hundreds of thousands of Buddhist practitioners in the world, they are not going to try to change the black and white robes of Catholics to the yellow and red robes of Buddhists. If there are some Westerners who like Buddhism, they are fortunate, and the Pope should rejoice instead of being fearful if someone's mind is made happy through Buddhism. If the Pope sees Westerners becoming good Buddhist monks or yogis, it is completely certain that it is not harmful but beneficial. Since the Pope is trying to convert all human beings to Catholicism, why should he be so concerned if a few Buddhists are "stirring up interest" (p. 85) in Buddhism in the West? It is unfair for the Pope to think that he and his priests can go all over the whole world to convert people to their religion but some small number of Buddhists cannot.

Even though the Pope does not accept Buddhism, instead of bringing a negative message about Buddhism to readers, he should consider that Buddhists are at least still human beings and belong to the world of humankind. He should show compassion rather than being contemptuous toward them, and he should try to create compatible phenomena among humankind. Since there are infinite beings, there are infinite ideas of what is best. One can only decide for oneself.

Each vehicle in Buddhism considers it nonvirtuous for a practitioner to build spiritual ego and then to be insulting to other religions. In Hinayana texts, Buddha Shakyamuni said that if someone builds spiritual ego and thinks, "Now I have attained the state of Arhat," it is a sign of not having attained that state. It is said in Mahayana sutra teachings that someone who has the conception that he has obtained high spiritual realization is influenced from his own dualistic, demonic habit. In Vajrayana Buddhism, it is said that one should not criticize or reject any other religions just to insult them, which would break the sixth vow of fourteen vows particular to the Vajrayana. Criticism should only be made with pure intention if there is a great reason for the benefit of other beings, such as their protection.

Each religion has its own logic, vision, and belief. Theoretical disagreements are just tiring. There is a saying that instead of carnivores and herbivores arguing with each other about what to eat, it is more convenient and comfortable for the family of carnivores to be with carnivores and for the family of herbivores to be with herbivores.

The Pope seems to be against Buddhism because it is a different religion than Christianity. However, even within Catholicism there are different orders, such as Benedictines, Franciscans, and Dominicans, and within Christianity there are different branches, such as Protestantism and Catholicism, and also there are different religions that share some of the same sacred writings, such as Judaism and Christianity. How can these differences be removed? Even regarding one Jesus, there are disputes as to whether Jesus has already come or is coming in the future. Depending on different beings' phenomena, his Christian time is earlier and his Jewish time is later. Since night and day happen at different times in the West than they do in the East, how can one expect to fix a single time for everyone? From the Buddhist point of view, time exists only according to the phenomena of sentient beings, and the phenomena of sentient beings is immeasurable and infinite. Even the mind of one single person has countless times and countless phenomena. Oneness cannot be made from substance. Oneness can be made only when dualistic habit is purified. Then all different times, directions, worlds, and gods can come together as one unification. That comes only with the correct point of view, prayer, and meditation.

After pointing to the difficulty of reciprocal contacts with Islamic fundamentalists, the Pope writes that

all the same, the Church remains always open to dialogue and cooperation. [p. 94]

Of course, I do not say this disrespectfully, but it seems that the Pope has two major fears in his book. One is that Islamic fundamentalists are going to cause a holy war. I hope that this worry will not be necessary, because although there may be some fundamentalists who would cause war, I hope that there are also many respectable holders of Islamic tradition who believe in peace. However, out of fear that fundamentalists will bomb everywhere, the Pope wants to be open to dialogue with them. Also, somehow the Pope knows that Buddhism is very mystical, so his other great fear is that many intelligent people will be drawn to it, including Westerners, and will change from Christianity, and therefore he tries to condemn Buddhism without logic so that his followers will not be aroused by the Buddhist tradition.

I am bewildered by the Pope's paradoxical way of openly and obviously insulting Buddhism. Although in one way it is seriously insulting, at the same time, I can see that the Pope has let a good thought suddenly emerge without examining it. Even if he threateningly shakes his scepter a little, he knows somehow that Buddhism is harmless, which is why he can say anything he wishes about it. So unnoticeably and unintentionally, the Pope has the positive conception that Buddhism will not hurt anyone. From the interference of the proof of this involuntary positive thought that squeezes in between his negative conceptions, the reasoning of what the Pope has said about Buddhism is self-defeated.

If I were in the Council, which

> has also called for the Church to have a dialogue with followers of the Prophet [p. 93],

I would think that one is not supposed to start an idea of having a dialogue between religions, which sounds like a politician's idea. If Christians just follow what Jesus said, keeping and continuously teaching the Ten Commandments, meditating, and thinking of God, it will not be against anyone even if there is not a dialogue with anyone.

According to the Mahayana, it is impossible to suppress Buddha nature since it exists intrinsically in each being's mind. It will manifest someday. What is truly impossible is to try to make it not occur. This causes it to occur more by alerting intelligent beings to wake up and think so that they can know who is wrong and who is right. Then they will join whoever they think is going in the right direction. If the Pope does not want Buddhism to appear because he does not want to lose Catholic followers, he should think instead that these followers are not going to give up God because God cannot be given up, since God is insubstantial. This is also true for the Holy Spirit, because it functions insubstantially, so many people cannot catch what it is within their material phenomena, and so they are not going to give it up. Jesus already left many wonderful histories, and for two thousand years, many followers have had faith in him, so the good habit of faith already exists. Other religions should be allowed to continue in their own way, which then makes the Catholic religion more powerful because of being more reasonably open. The Pope has to be quiet. If he talks more, what he fears will occur more.

The Pope says,

> Man affirms himself most completely by giving of himself. This is the fulfillment of the commandment of love. [p. 202]

Then, as an act of generosity, why can't the Pope give Buddhists the chance to be Buddhists? Since

> the Council says that the Holy Spirit works effectively even outside of the visible structure of the Church [p. 81],

and the Pope says,

> I have been convinced of this on numerous occasions, both while visiting the countries of the Far East and while meeting representatives of those religions [p. 81],

why can't he think that Buddhism may be a manifestation of the Holy Spirit? Even if the Pope believes that the only salvation is through Jesus, he can still acknowledge, as he quotes the Council saying, that other religions often reflect a ray of truth that enlightens all men (p. 80).

The Pope must know that it will not be beneficial even for Christians if he talks about how Buddhism is bad and Christianity is good. He may say this among followers who agree with his views, but if he fearfully blurts misunderstandings publicly without understanding Buddhism, he can destroy people's faith in what he says and in his own doctrine through his errors. Since there are many stupid people and many intelligent people, it is uncertain how what he says will be interpreted and whether it will be harmful or beneficial for his own church if he talks in this way.

Modern people like change. Although the Pope seems to be motivated by the fear that Catholics will become interested in Buddhism, so he has written about Buddhism in order to discourage and prevent them from changing their religion, sometimes one really has to be careful about an internal situation instead of trying to prevent an external threat. The Pope needs to be careful about what to say even among Christians. Also, if the protection of one's own position is too intensive, especially at the expense of others, it is not certain whether it will result in protection or self-destruction. As Dharmabhadra said,

If a windstorm comes, trees can protect each other.
If a fire comes, trees can become each other's enemies.

When the Pope refers to the Buddha's "enlightenment" (pp. 85–87), it is clearly implied by the quotation marks that Buddhist enlightenment is not considered to be actual enlightenment by the Pope. Of course, Buddhists are not hoping that the Pope is going to accept Buddhism, and they also are not going to lose their own faith in Buddhism if the Pope is disparaging toward it. But one is not supposed to go so far to denounce Buddhism. As he knows, even though there have been rulers in our generation such as Stalin and Mao who tried to stop all religion and massacred millions, intangible spirituality increased again after their deaths. Likewise, even though some may try to destroy other religions in order to expand their own religions, different spiritual habits among different beings will still grow because spirituality, which inherently exists in the minds of beings, cannot end. Immaterial spirituality cannot be destroyed, like a natural spring whose water continues to arise and flow out even if someone tries to cover it over with earth, so it is always better to encourage it than to try to suppress it.

Every religious leader should try to create peace in the world instead of contradiction and conflict.

The Pope writes,

> It is not inappropriate to caution those Christians who enthusiastically welcome certain ideas originating in the religious traditions of the Far East—for example, techniques and methods of meditation and ascetical practice. In some quarters, these have become fashionable and are accepted rather uncritically. [pp. 89–90]

Does that mean that it is all right with the Pope if Buddhists accept them? The Pope indirectly recognizes that people are somehow attracted to Buddhism with its ability to cause peace and not conflict, with his continuing concern that Christians will doubt Christianity and turn to Buddhism. But the way a religion draws its followers to it cannot be based on invalidating other religions. The Pope should pray for Buddhism to prosper, instead of trying to change other religions to his own religion and worrying that the harmless, purely beneficial qualities of Buddhism will blossom and flourish.

The Pope says,

> First one should know one's own spiritual heritage well and consider whether it is right to set it aside lightly. [p. 90]

However, the Pope goes everywhere in the world trying to convince the followers of other religions to set aside their own spiritual heritages lightly and become Catholic. Naturally, he is loyal to his own tradition, but he should not impose it on others who are loyal to theirs.

The Pope says,

> The call for a great relaunching of evangelization enters again and again into the present life of the Church in a number of ways. [p. 105]

Many great leaders of eternalist religions have been concerned with conversion. But too much emphasis on trying to convert each other can cause no religion at all by precipitating divisive conflicts that lead to hatred and slaughter, causing living beings to turn into corpses. All religious leaders, instead of making too much of an effort to convert followers, should be more concerned with causing negative antireligious results. Just being against different religions with excessive judgments about others comes from a dualistic point of view and not from a pure, spiritual source. The focus on conversion comes from too much of a wish for victory for oneself and one's own side, and for the demolishment of others and other sides. But to defeat others and benefit oneself has nothing to do with religion. Regarding the world's religious leaders who sell their religions in order to manipulate the world, provoking people and stirring up antagonism, Shantideva prayed:

> May you liberate all these beasts who are eating each other.

I have only answered the questions I was asked by referring to the Pope's own words about Buddhism. I did not have an intention to be disrespectful toward Catholicism. I hope and pray that this answer to the Pope's inaccurate ideas about Buddhism will not be damaging for the Pope's followers. I have written this for the benefit of Christians and Buddhists, and I pray that the Pope will live long to further the development of spirituality, without conflict or disturbance between individuals, groups, or religions due to their misinterpretation of other doctrines, and that the followers of all religions can become harmonious.

In the future, please do not blame the Polish people who asked me to write an answer to the Pope's fiction about Buddhism. They were broadminded to want to reveal the truth for the benefit of others.

Since the Pope teaches millions of people, I hope he will understand his misunderstandings of the Buddhist point of view. He should publish his corrections of his misunderstandings so his followers will understand Buddhism correctly instead of misunderstanding the Buddhist view of experience, enlightenment, evil, good, reality, detachment, love, compassion, mysticism, and union. To make a request of the Pope, using some of the words of the poem of Saint John of the Cross:

> To arrive at what now the Pope does not enjoy about
> Buddhism, he must go into a Buddhist temple.
> To reach what the Pope does not know about Buddhism,
> he must go where he will know the state of
> omniscience.
> To come into possession of what the Pope does not have
> about Buddhism, he must go to the state of the creator
> who can create anything.

I was positive about the Pope before, I am positive now, and I will be positive in the future, and this will not change or diminish through this book that he has written. Since some years ago when I saw the Pope on television teaching about faith, compassion, and love, as my friends around me know, I admired the Pope, who was helping the world. I only answered, at people's requests, what the Pope clearly said about Buddhism. It is as though the Pope suddenly vomited insolently and uncontrollably in a cathedral, so I hastily had to clean it, as the Polish people asked me to do.

Each religion decides that whatever beliefs they hold to be true are the highest point of view. So that is not a problem, and no one will be disappointed about being considered lower by anyone else, since they believe their own way is superior in the same way that the Pope thinks that Christianity is superior. No one thinks they are inferior, even if they are called that by others. But when deciding what to believe, one should not try to efface what another has decided to believe, since everyone decides what they believe is true according to their own faculties. If one talks too much, it naturally causes more talk and dualistic discussion at an intellectual level, which is different from spiritual practice that causes the speechlessness of inexpressible wisdom. What seems low and impure and what seems high and pure is all habit within a relative point of view. What is actually precious is beginningless, nondualistic wisdom, in which everything becomes the manifestation of the display of wisdom mind.

I am very happy to hear that the Pope has met with the great leaders of other religions. From their continual meetings, this history of trying to win over others can be reduced, and pure faith and love can increase, to unite all beings in the universe in the fully enlightened great sphere of nonsubstantial oneness.

I am very grateful to the Pope for being like a hard-hitting drumstick that has given me the good opportunity to be like a drum myself, resonating with the sound of profound Dharma. I am grateful to the Pope for yelling with negative words in a valley, letting me return the answer of its transformation into the positive echo of Buddhist hymns. I am grateful for American freedom of speech, so I can speak freely. I am grateful for American freedom of religion, so I can offer a garland of fragrant amaranthine flowers of the speech of the Buddhas to the Pope when he crosses the threshold of hope. I am grateful to hear the Pope is the messenger of God, so I can wait to someday hear his infallible message.

Whether or not crossing the threshold of hope, may the fragrance of the flowers of wisdom blessings of the Buddhas and Bodhisattvas fill all places.

NOTES

Introduction

1. Hinayana (Tib. Theg.pa dman.pa). See note 3.
2. Vehicle (Tib. Theg.pa; Skt. yana). Way of lifting up from lower states to higher spiritual states.
3. Hinayana (Tib. Theg.pa dman.pa). The foundational vehicle of Buddhism.
4. Mahayana (Tib. Theg.pa chhen.po). The greater vehicle of Buddhism.
5. Vajrayana (Tib. rDo.rje theg.pa). The vehicle of the teaching of the great way of carrying from lower states to higher spiritual states.

CHAPTER 1: Experience and Enlightenment

1. Causal vehicle (Tib. rGyu yi theg.pa). The vehicle that teaches that cause leads to result.
2. Bodhisattva (Tib. Byang.chhub sems.dpa'). Compassionate sublime being.
3. Passions (Tib. nyon.mong). There are countless passions, which can be synthesized in the five root passions of ignorance, desire, jealousy, anger, and pride.
4. Resultant vehicle (Tib. 'Bras.bu'i theg.pa). The vehicle in

which the result is used as the path to attain fully enlightened Buddhahood, which is faster than the causal vehicle.

5. Elements (Tib. Khams). The ordinary flesh, breath, warmth, body fluids including blood, and consciousness correspond to the ordinary outer elements of earth, air, fire, water, and space. Mind is based on these elements. Within the body, earth and water are contained. Within speech, air and fire are contained. Within consciousness, space is contained. The wisdom elements are naturally hidden within the ordinary elements. From the lack of recognition of the actual, light wisdom elements, the ordinary outer and inner elements occur. The ordinary outer and inner elements rely on each other and eventually decay and disappear. After leaving the elements of the body at death, because mind is continuous, one must unavoidably take form again according to one's karma unless one transforms the ordinary elements into wisdom elements by praying, worshipping, abiding in emptiness, and meditating.

6. Contributing circumstances (Tib. rKyen). Conditions such as soil, water, and sunlight, which function with root circumstances, such as seeds, to produce results within substance; or at a spiritual level, conditions such as hearing the teachings of Buddha or seeing Buddha, which connect with the root circumstance of Buddha nature in order for it to blossom to the result of Buddhahood.

7. Root circumstances (Tib. rGyu). Basic conditions, such as seeds, which function with contributing circumstances, such as soil, water, and sunlight, to produce results within substance; or at a spiritual level, the basis of Buddha nature. Just as if there are no contributing circumstances of soil, water, and sunlight, a seed cannot grow into a plant, even though there is the root circumstance of Buddha nature, if no contributing circumstances connect with it such as the teachings of Buddha,

it cannot blossom. So it is necessary for both root and contributing circumstances to function together to reach the result and to unite for the attainment of fully enlightened Buddhahood, which is beyond root and contributing circumstances and which becomes oneness that is beyond relying on two things or any conditions.

8. Nirvana (Tib. Myang.'das). The state in which samsaric phenomena have ceased, according to the Hinayana vehicle, from the personal realization of the I-less point of view. All enemies of the passions, which are the creators of suffering, are exhausted in peace from the power of samadhi.

CHAPTER 2: Evil, Good, and Reality

1. Dharma (Tib. Chhos). The holding of phenomena. All dharma can be contained within the two categories of worldly phenomena, which holds all phenomena from dualistic mind, creating ordinary phenomena again; and holy Dharma, which holds all the display of wisdom and unclinging phenomena from nondualistic wisdom mind, manifesting Buddhas. In this case, the reference is to holy Dharma.

2. Interdependent links (Tib. rTen.'brel). The twelve interdependent links of causation are ignorance (Tib. Ma.rig.pa); perception (Tib. 'Du.byed); consciousness (Tib. rNam.par shes.pa); name and form (Tib. Ming.gzugs); the six senses (Tib. sKye.mchhed drug); contact (Tib. Reg.pa); feeling (Tib. Tshor.ba); desire (Tib. Sred.pa); grasping (Tib. Len.pa); coming into being in samsaric existence (Tib. Srid.pa); rebirth (Tib. sKye.ba); and old age and death (Tib. rGa.shi).

3. Relative truth (Tib. Kun.rdzob bden.pa). The truth which relies on phenomena that depend on and are related to one another.

4. Karma (Tib. Las). According to the causal vehicle, karma

is the activity of cause and result. According to the resultant vehicle, it is unnecessary to divide cause from result. By recognizing the divisionless, pure nature of immeasurable existence and the wisdom energy of stainless Buddhas, all activity becomes the spontaneous display of Dharmakaya.

5. General and personal phenomena (Tib. gShen.snang; Rang.snang). General phenomena is the group agreement of the shared perceptions of whatever phenomena beings have in common with each other, such as seeing and hearing the same sights and sounds or thinking in the same way. Personal phenomena is the particular phenomena of an individual. General and personal phenomena depend on each other, since all general phenomena come from personal phenomena and belong to relative truth. If personal phenomena are purified, impure general phenomena also become pure. The recognition of wisdom is beyond all conceptions of outer general phenomena and inner personal phenomena.

6. Samsara (Tib. 'Khor.ba). All deluded existence originating from dualistic mind.

7. Bodhicitta (Tib. Byang.chhub nying.po). The aspiration to help all sentient beings attain liberation from the suffering of samsara.

8. Six paramitas (Tib. Phar.phyin drug). The six paramitas are generosity (Tib. sByin.pa), morality (Tib. Tshul. khrims), patience (Tib. bZod.pa), diligence (Tib. brTson.'grus), meditation (Tib. bSam.gtan), and wisdom (Tib. Shes.rab).

9. Skandhas (Tib. Phung.po). These are the five aggregates of form (Tib. gZugs), feeling (Tib. Tshor.ba), perception (Tib. 'Du.shes), intention (Tib. 'Du.byed), and consciousness (Tib. rNams.par.shes.pa'i phung.po).

10. Dharmakaya (Tib. Chhos.sku). Completely pure formless form.

CHAPTER 3: Breaking Ties to Reality

1. Arhat (Tib. dGra.bchom.pa). One who has subdued the enemy of the passions, or attained nirvana according to the Hinayana doctrine.

CHAPTER 4: Indifference, Detachment, and Love

1. Sambhogakaya (Tib. Longs.sku). Immeasurable qualities of flawless, inconceivable, desireless exaltation emanation form.
2. Nirmanakaya (Tib. sPrul.sku). Unobstructed miraculous emanation form.

CHAPTER 6: Creation

1. Eight leisures (Tib. Dal.ba brgyad). These are not to be born as a being in the hell realm, in the hungry ghost realm, or in the animal realm, where beings are suffering from karmic results without the leisure to follow Dharma; not to be born as a savage whose mind does not turn toward Dharma; not to be born as long-living gods whose enjoyment of karmic results eventually is exhausted and who are reborn in samsaric suffering; not to be born as a heretic with no opportunity to develop faith in Dharma; not to be born when Buddhas do not appear; and not to be born in mute stupidity, unable to understand Dharma.
2. Ten opportunities (Tib. 'Byor.ba bchu). These are the five endowments that rely on oneself, which are to obtain a precious human body, to be born in a central land where Dharma exists, to have perfect faculties, not to be engaged in activities that are against Dharma, and to have faith in Dharma; and the five endowments that rely on others, which are that Buddha has appeared, Buddha has taught Dharma, Buddha's teaching continues during one's own time, Buddha's teachings are followed, and to be guided by a teacher.

CHAPTER 8: Mysticism

1. Shamatha (Tib. Zhi.gnas). The meditative state of tranquil stillness.
2. Vipasana (Tib. Lhag.thong). The meditative state of sublime seeing.

ALSO BY THINLEY NORBU

A Cascading Waterfall of Nectar

The open and natural words of Thinley Norbu, uncomplicated by scholarly elaboration, flow here in the tradition of the direct transmissions of Buddhas and Bodhisattvas of the past. Through commentary on the Preliminary Practices (Ngöndrö) prayer from the treasure text of the great master Tragtung Düdjom Lingpa, insights into many central practices emerge in order to deepen understanding of the foundations of Vajrayana Buddhism.

*Magic Dance: The Display of Self-Nature
of the Five Wisdom Dakinis*

This is a unique and powerful presentation of the teachings of Tibetan Buddhism on the five elements: earth, water, air, fire, and space. Through teachings, stories, and his distinctive use of language, Thinley Norbu relates how the energies of the elements manifest within our everyday world in individual behavior and group traditions, relationships and solitude, medicine and art.

*The Small Golden Key to the Treasure of the Various
Essential Necessities of General and Extraordinary
Buddhist Dharma*

In *The Small Golden Key*, Thinley Norbu explains in simple, concise language the important ideas and practices of Buddhism, with special attention to the Vajrayana teachings of Tibetan Buddhism. He discusses the origins of Buddhism in India and its spread to Tibet; the important lineages of Tibetan Buddhism, with emphasis on the Nyingma school; the differences between the Hinayana, Mahayana, and Vajrayana teachings; the outstanding features of the Mahayana; and some of the special qualities and practices of the Vajrayana.

*White Sail: Crossing the Waves of Ocean Mind
to the Serene Continent of the Triple Gems*

Buddhism teaches that enlightenment is our natural state; the problem is that we do not recognize this state, owing to the mind's confusion about its true nature. Thinley Norbu presents the Buddhist view in a way meant to clear up misconceptions and awaken the reader's innate wisdom.

Printed in the United States
by Baker & Taylor Publisher Services